Understanding Site in Design Pedagogy

This book examines diverse ways of questioning, critiquing, and communicating site in the creative process of architecture, interior design, urban planning, and historical and cultural studies. The authors use the term *site* to connote a series of complex, established, or pre-existing conditions – a setting, an atmosphere, an area – to read, to interpret, to relate to, and to engage with, to redefine, or to create in relation to a design prompt. By acknowledging, accommodating, and empowering the physical, intellectual, and cultural characteristics of a site, students question its history, boundaries, posture, and situational aspects. Such inquiries promote a deeper appreciation of a site and thus help students to acknowledge its capacity to influence design throughout the iterative creative process.

Understanding Site in Design Pedagogy adds to the body of literature on design studio pedagogy by presenting a collection of essays that challenge normative assumptions about what defines a site and its distinctive qualities. It poses a series of pedagogical questions for how sites might be diversely interpreted and introduced to design students. This study offers chapters that speak to site, memory, and lived experience; multi-scalar thinking about site; connecting to site through sensory phenomenon in interior design; alternate ways of engaging site for learning sustainable principles; and introducing unorthodox forms of site as the impetus to creative endeavours. It offers innovative approaches to scholarship of teaching and learning with respect to diverse readings of site within design education.

Sean Burns is an Assistant Professor of Architecture at Ball State University specializing in architectural design, with an emphasis on foundations of design and beginner architectural education, as well as structural principles and behavioural analysis. Sean holds a professional Bachelor of Architecture degree from Kent State University and a post-professional Master of Architecture degree, with specialization in Architectural Design and Theory, from the University of Pennsylvania. Sean's current research concentrates on how the conditions of a site, both above and beyond the demarcation of the earth's surface and qualitative substance composition, might be influential agents throughout the architectural design process. This research is grounded in the writings and lessons of architectural theorists and other allied disciplines and applied through the methodological approaches to design as evident in his courses.

Matthew Wilson is an Assistant Professor at Ball State University. As an intellectual historian, his research focuses on political thought, sociology, and the built environment. Wilson holds a master's degree from the Architectural Association and a PhD from the University of London. He has taught aspects of social and environmental justice; post-colonial architectural history; critical theory, psychogeography, and utopian studies; architecture, gender, and race; and design research methods. He is an African American Studies faculty affiliate at Ball State. As a designer and scholar, his creations have been exhibited in Mexico, China, the United Kingdom, the United Arab Emirates, Turkey, Japan, and across the United States and Europe. Wilson was visiting scholar at *École des hautes études en sciences sociales* in Paris, France, and senior lecturer at the University for the Creative Arts in Canterbury, England. Wilson is the author of *Moralising Space: The Utopian Urbanism of the British Positivists, 1855–1920* (2018) and *Richard Congreve: Positivist Politics, the Victorian Press, and the British Empire* (2021). His current project is *Positivism and the Origins of Feminism: Nineteenth-century British Women Philosophers*.

Routledge Focus on Design Pedagogy
Series Editor: Graham Cairns

The Routledge Focus on Design Pedagogy series provides the reader with the latest scholarship for instructors who educate designers. The series publishes research from across the globe and covers areas as diverse as beginning design and foundational design, architecture, product design, interior design, fashion design, landscape architecture, urban design, and architectural conservation and historic preservation. By making these studies available to the worldwide academic community, the series aims to promote quality design education.

Fluid Space and Transformational Learning
Kyriaki Tsoukala

Progressive Studio Pedagogy
Examples from Architecture and Allied Design Fields
Edited by Charlie Smith

Emerging Practices in Architectural Pedagogy
Accommodating an Uncertain Future
Edited by Laura Sanderson and Sally Stone

For more information about this series, please visit: https://www.routledge.com/architecture/series/RFDP

Understanding Site in Design Pedagogy

Edited by Sean Burns and Matthew Wilson

LONDON AND NEW YORK

First published 2023
by Routledge
4 Park Square, Milton Park, Abingdon, Oxon OX14 4RN

and by Routledge
605 Third Avenue, New York, NY 10158

Routledge is an imprint of the Taylor & Francis Group, an informa business

© 2023 selection and editorial matter, Sean Burns and Matthew Wilson; individual chapters, the contributors

The right of Sean Burns and Matthew Wilson to be identified as the author[/s] of the editorial material, and of the authors for their individual chapters, has been asserted in accordance with sections 77 and 78 of the Copyright, Designs and Patents Act 1988.

All rights reserved. No part of this book may be reprinted or reproduced or utilised in any form or by any electronic, mechanical, or other means, now known or hereafter invented, including photocopying and recording, or in any information storage or retrieval system, without permission in writing from the publishers.

Trademark notice: Product or corporate names may be trademarks or registered trademarks, and are used only for identification and explanation without intent to infringe.

British Library Cataloguing-in-Publication Data
A catalogue record for this book is available from the British Library

ISBN: 978-1-032-34542-0 (hbk)
ISBN: 978-1-032-34543-7 (pbk)
ISBN: 978-1-003-32272-6 (ebk)

DOI: 10.4324/9781003322726

Typeset in Times New Roman
by KnowledgeWorks Global Ltd.

Contents

List of Figures	ix
Acknowledgements	xi
List of Contributors	xii

Introduction   1
SEAN BURNS AND MATTHEW WILSON

1 Mutable Atmospheres: A Lens In to Look Out   10
CHELSEA D. LIMBIRD

2 Going to Places and Staying at Home: Reflections on Critical Cartography and Desktop Documentation in Online Education   29
EMILY BERESKIN AND NATACHA QUINTERO GONZÁLEZ

3 Sites of Alternate Origin: Design Ideation Under a New Austerity   51
SEAN BURNS AND MATTHEW WILSON

4 Sensorial Strategies: A Phenomenological Approach Connecting Site to Interior Design   79
LISA PHILLIPS

| 5 | Touring Spaceship Earth | 102 |

LISA CLAYPOOL

Conclusion 119

SEAN BURNS AND MATTHEW WILSON

Index 122

List of Figures

1.1	"Atmospheres of the Day, The story of underpasses and viaducts" by Jing Wang.	18
1.2	"Adaptation Case Study, Storefront for Art and Architecture, Concept and Experience" by Xueni Hu.	22
1.3	"Adaptation Case Study, University Metro Station, Site Section" by Yanya Mei.	23
1.4	"Mutable Sites, Sensory Upgrade, Before/After Collage" by Savannah Shi.	25
2.1	'Sugar wonderland – from the farmland to the supermarket shelf' (Daniel Cardué, Theres Marthaler, Natalie Schubert, and Lukas Teschner, 2021).	36
2.2	'The architectures of tea plantations in Darjeeling, India' (Julia Fritsche, Laurin Roman Henklein, Julia Theite Piro, and Leonard Zappe, 2021).	37
2.3	Desktop documentary with fictitious website on regional shops (Chloe Angot, Charlene Caspar, Patrick Kühlwein, Natalie Schuberg, and Lukas Teschner, 2021).	42
2.4	Desktop documentary with self-created website and fictitious interview (Julia Hübner, Belinda Kergel, Paul Lambrecht, and Gianna Mund, 2021).	42
3.1	Empire Quarry by Alex Tyson.	59
3.2	Room and [bill]Board by Camden Hochgesang and Brian Cruz.	61
3.3	Po-Mo Church by Allison Gerardot, Roberto Medina, Camden Hochgesang, and Derek Burks.	63
3.4	(a) top row, 'Instigating Mass' by Jake Nolan, and (b) bottom two rows, 'Huis Clos' by Jack Leibham, Carson Vaal, Mini Liard, and Keith Carrasquilla.	66

3.5	The 'Bloody Sunday Memorial' by J. Canaday, B. Williams, and D. Yao; 'Memorial for the Charleston Church Massacre' by N. Conley and N. Porter; and 'Remembering the Baltimore Uprising' by J. Daniyam, A. Strayer, and B. Williams.	70
4.1	Therme Vals in Switzerland by architect, Peter Zumthor. Photo by lauravr/Shutterstock.com.	83
4.2	Sensory maps created by student, Kaylie Siwy, F'20 term at Thomas Jefferson University.	86
4.3	Process & final work by student, Charisse Reid, F'20 term at Thomas Jefferson University.	92
4.4	Final work by student, Ashley Hurst, F'21 term at Thomas Jefferson University.	94
5.1	Jingyu Zhang. Big Thousand World (Daqian shijie 大千世界). 2021. Unmounted handscroll, xuan paper and ink; 40.6 × 482.6 cm. Courtesy of the artist. Photograph by author.	103
5.2	Émile Gallé. Vase with insect. Layered glass, h: 16 cm, maximum w: 15 cm. Courtesy of the Museum of Applied Arts, Budapest.	113

Acknowledgements

The creators of this book would like to relay many thanks to Caroline Church at Routledge/Taylor and Francis and to Graham Cairns at Architecture, Media, Politics, Society (AMPS) for their encouragement and support during the making of this book. We would also like to offer deep thanks to our peer reviewers for their constructive suggestions and all the universities and schools affiliated with the authors of this study. Finally, we offer our gratitude to the students whose hard work is presented in this book.

List of Contributors

Emily Bereskin is a senior researcher at the Department of Urban Planning at BTU Cottbus. Prior to joining BTU, Dr. Bereskin worked on two EU-HERA projects at the Kulturwissenschaftliches Institut Essen and at the Technische Universität Berlin's Habitat Unit. She was also a DFG (German Research Foundation) postdoctoral fellow at the TU Berlin's Center for Metropolitan Studies and remains a research associate of the institute. She received her doctorate in 2012 from Bryn Mawr College.

Lisa Claypool is an associate professor of the History of Art, Design, and Visual Culture at the University of Alberta. She is finishing up a book manuscript that asks how design in early twentieth-century China encourages us to see and engage with the natural world. She has curated numerous exhibitions, including *ecoArt China* (ecoartchina.html), *China's Imperial Modern*, *China Urban*, and has published in the journals *positions: east asia cultures critique*, *The Journal of Asian Studies*, and *Yishu: The Journal of Contemporary Chinese Art*, among others.

Chelsea D. Limbrid is an architectural designer, artist, writer, and educator based in New York City and Rhode Island. Her work focuses on processes of narrative, memory, and presence, as generators for line, word, image, and experience. She teaches design studio, representation, and interdisciplinary theory courses at Pratt Institute, Parsons the Newschool for Design, and Brown University and has held teaching positions at the Rhode Island School of Design, and the China Academy of Art. She has exhibited drawing, photography, and artist books in New York, Rhode Island, Philadelphia, and Tokyo and has published prose, poetry, and design projects internationally. Chelsea graduated from Brown University with a double concentration in Economics and Architectural Studies and received her Master of Architecture degree from the Rhode Island School of Design.

Lisa Phillips, NCIDQ, is an associate professor of Interior Design at Thomas Jefferson University in Philadelphia. She has a Bachelor of Architecture degree and Master of Education degree, both from Temple University. Ms. Phillips has over 20 years of experience teaching in interior design and has won numerous teaching awards, including DesignIntelligence's 25 Most Admired Educators for 2017–18. She currently teaches design studios, visualization courses, and capstone research and programming. Her areas of research include design andragogy and the study of materiality as it relates to sensory input and the user experience.

Natacha S. Quintero González is a research and teaching assistant at the Department of Urban Planning at BTU Cottbus-Senftenberg, and a doctoral candidate at the TU Berlin. She received training as an architect at the Universidad Central de Venezuela (UCV) and studied for her MSc in Urban Development at the TU Berlin Campus El Gouna. Her PhD research focuses on human-nature relations within spontaneous, auto-produced, and self-organized urban spaces in Latin America. She is particularly interested in how relational perspectives together with collaborative, visual, and narrative research methods can contribute to social-ecological knowledge production.

Introduction

Sean Burns and Matthew Wilson

Within the context of the cultural production of space, the word 'site' is a vessel that contains various meanings. Graphic designers and writers might consider site as the intersection in which the mind communicates with words and graphics on the surface of the screen or the page. For industrial designers and fashion designers, it might be the place where the mind coordinates materials to fit, protect, or enhance the body. For landscape architects, interior designers, planners, and architects, it might be the atmosphere in which the mind aggregates materials between the earth and sky to suit the body and other designed objects.

Rather curiously, the emphasis on thinking and meaning is less evident than doing in the etymology of the word site. As a verb, site means to fix or to build something in a particular place. It dates to the late sixteenth century. As a noun, the word emerged in late Middle English from Anglo-Norman French, or from Latin *situs,* meaning 'local position'. It denotes 'a place where a particular event or activity is occurring or has occurred' according to the Oxford English Dictionary. This book seeks to draw on the connotations of site as the intersection of theory and practice. It aims to show the relevance of this concept of site in design education—to recenter conversations about the role of design in contemporary society.

It is not uncommon, for instance, to see hyperbolic criticisms from environmentalists who rail against design because 'the earth is burning'. Equally so, disillusioned academic administrators might, and shockingly have, muttered 'just let them [students] go off and destroy the planet'. Such commentaries point to a specific way of thinking about climate change and the potentially detrimental effects of the architectural education-industrial complex. They speak to ways of dealing with site—as either something sacred and to leave untouched and thus neglect or something to treat with reckless abandon. Neither narrative speaks to cultural responsibility or social justice.

DOI: 10.4324/9781003322726-1

There is indeed a growing body of scholarship that offers histories, theories, methods, and practices related to site and place in design pedagogy.[1] Laura Sanderson and Sally Stone's fine study *Emerging Practices in Architectural Pedagogy* (2021), for instance, offers a collection of case studies that explore participatory methods for teaching design studio. They aim to link together education and practice by having students address real-world issues they will face as professionals. The study covers such design pedagogy problems as how the profession will have to lead cross-disciplinary teams to adapt and to develop radical solutions to the complex demands of climate change and rapid densification.[2]

Kyna Leski's brilliant book *The Storm of Creativity* (2020), meanwhile, likens site to an iterative design event, where one storms through various dynamic stages, ranges of motion, and intensities in the creative process. Leski argues that students should undergo a course of unlearning specific predisposed notions of the creative process. This method encourages experimentation and promotes students and educators to avoid linear design processes across various creative fields. Leski's storm of creativity embraces chaos, confusion, doubt, and struggle, as opportunities to open new realms of production in various design disciplines. Pedagogical examples are presented from various fields of practice, including art, architecture, and poetry.[3]

Along similar lines, Genevieve S. Baudoin's phenomenal study *Interpreting Site* (2015) explores the act of reading, translating, and representing a site's contextual embedded messages as an influential process toward the creation and communication of a designer's intentions: to shape experiences through informed interventions. Baudoin introduces theory, analysis, and case studies to demonstrate how a given site's implications, history, and influential forces are acknowledged and appreciated throughout the architectural design process. The book's content is applicable to students of architecture and experienced practitioners, for the text stresses individuality for a designer's appreciation of site constraints and parameters toward the motivation and implicative consequences of their design decisions. Baudoin's study considers site as an impetus to the design process.[4]

Looking back to the modernists, Ilka and Andreas Ruby's ingenious book *Groundscapes* (2002) affirms the rediscovery of 'the ground' as a significant factor in design practice. The Rubys argue that the ground is no longer a stable or neutral medium. It is a dynamic entity that fluctuates and changes. Contemporary designers should, in turn, develop strategies for integrating it into the creative process. Thematically organized, the book offers case studies that examine different strategies for addressing the ground plane. It begins with the modernist approach of 'lifted off the ground' and carries on to demonstrate contemporary designers' interests in the 'inflated', 'carved', and 'stacked' grounds alongside other methods of challenging the figure-ground condition.[5]

Among other notable books on this subject, David Leatherbarrow's astute study *Uncommon Ground* (2002) offers a critique of modernist thinking on architecture as an object distinct from that is emancipated from site conditions. *Uncommon Ground* argues that designers should better integrate building designs with their physical surroundings. Leatherbarrow challenges the assumptions of modernists who have asserted that technological advancements meant they could disregard or ignore a building's natural surroundings. Siting and construction, argues Leatherbarrow, should be treated as having a shared interest in the design process. Leatherbarrow describes the role of boundary in architecture and how it relates to the physical qualities of a site. Topography, argues Leatherbarrow, should be understood as a medium in design.[6]

While such admirable works discuss the significance of site in the design process, this book takes pause to reflect on its broader connotations. Over the past few decades, the world of design pedagogy has shifted from a focus on drawing, design, and representation to the act of making by hand or intelligent machine. This book poses the question: what if the site in which we speak is of an intangible quality but nonetheless has a 'place' in the world? Drawing on an immense body of scholarship, we too are concerned with locality, with 'interpreting data', with 'tectonic sensibility', with 'current technology', and with creations that evoke memory and meaning in daily life.[7] Yet if one rejects metanarratives and adheres to poststructuralist notions of multiple, localized worlds, we also hold that intangible, or virtual, sites have value in the act of teaching and making.

This study thus wants something more from the word site. It speaks of multi-disciplinary approaches to pedagogies in spatial design; the role, responsibilities, and influences of site within design education; notions of site beyond the realm of the discipline of architecture; and it questions whether site can be more than physical but conceptual, virtual, remote, or online.[8] Moreover, this book stresses site as a situation for critical reflection and mental activity that engrains geometry with cultural significance. It speaks to creating and teaching about things worth cultural value, worth protecting, and worth caring for. It emerges from observations of design students and academics who sometimes operate on the assumption that site simply amounts to a concrete setting: a vacant urban plot, a desolate wood, a strip mall, a campus green, and the like. They feel they can ignore site because, in a modernist fashion, architecture is an object 'detached from the ground'. Or, alternately, they view site as having no value and thus they view it through a colonialist lens: as a tabula rasa on which to inscribe their totalizing visions.[9]

With an interest in reflecting about what site means, this book seeks to encourage an exchange of ideas from different disciplines about the concept. It thus examines diverse ways of questioning, critiquing, and communicating site in the creative process in architecture, interior design, urban planning, philosophy, social and environmental justice, literature, and historical and cultural studies. By acknowledging, accommodating, and empowering the physical, intellectual, and cultural characteristics of a site, students question its history, its boundaries, its posture, and its situational aspects. Such inquiries promote a deeper appreciation of a site and thus help students to acknowledge its capacity to influence design throughout the iterative, creative process.

Thus as a collection of essays, this book challenges siloed disciplinary assumptions about what defines a site and its distinctive qualities. It poses a series of pedagogical questions for how sites might be diversely interpreted and introduced to design students. As such, this study examines notions of introducing sensory phenomena about site while in remote locations, unorthodox notions of site as the impetus to creativity, managing and maintaining the finite qualities of site, and activating site as a participant throughout the design process. This book offers approaches to the scholarship of teaching and learning with respect to diverse readings of site within design education. The motivation is to enable one to develop alternatives to traditional notions of site and innovative and progressive design studio pedagogy.

The first chapter, entitled 'Mutable Atmospheres', by the architectural designer, artist, writer, and educator Chelsea Limbird centers on experience and memory as foundations to generate spatial proposals for the adaptation of interiors, architecture, and the urban realm. Limbird argues that investigations into the personal and local have the potential to reveal shared truths. When paralleled and scaffolded through time-based representational processes, these proposals for space synchronize with lived experience and the ever-evolving reality of the environment, materials, culture, and human relationships.

Thereafter this book features a chapter by the senior researcher at the Department of Urban Planning at BTU Cottbus Dr. Emily

Bereskin and Natacha S. Quintero González, research and teaching assistant at the Department of Urban Planning at BTU Cottbus-Senftenberg and doctoral candidate at the TU Berlin. Their chapter entitled 'Going to Places and Staying at Home: Critical Reflections on Thematic Cartography and Desktop Documentation in Online Education' examines experimental online formats as alternatives to traditional place-bound approaches to urban planning education. The traditional notion of 'site' is replaced with a relational understanding of global, regional, and urban systems centered around the home. Using the investigation of the global-food system as an example, this chapter presents two digital methodologies—thematic cartography and desktop documentation—that enable students to link everyday practices in the home with spatial processes happening 'elsewhere' while simultaneously demanding that the students grapple with the epistemology of digital learning, research, and presentation.

The third chapter offers a presentation of design studio thinking under the rubric 'Sites of Alternate Origin' by Ball State assistant professors Sean Burns and Matthew Wilson. The chapter examines a series of architectural design projects that encourage students to envision, design, and fabricate their own 'site' based on hermeneutic approaches to various theoretical and philosophical texts. As such, these projects ask the students to abandon their preconceived notions about the sequence of observing, documenting, and reacting to a physical site as a formal procedure for creating an architectural intervention. Collectively, the projects exemplified an array of efforts to expand the view of architecture's role as a mediating article throughout the design process, toward demonstrating a profound relationship between an edifice and its accommodating field. This chapter offers examples of this pedagogical approach and argues that when online students are prompted to consider alternatives to 'site', they are presented with new interdisciplinary opportunities that expand their horizons.

The fourth chapter is 'Sensorial Strategies: A Phenomenological Approach Connecting Site to Interior Design' by Lisa Phillips, NCIDQ, who is an associate professor of Interior Design at Thomas Jefferson University in Philadelphia. This chapter will focus on sensorial analysis of exterior environments and how this data can inform the interior design decision-making process. How can awareness of external olfactory, auditory and tactile data add to the making of internal places and spaces? Tranquility pods, designed as a studio project by junior-level interior design students, serve as examples to present this methodology, highlighting strategies that take advantage of context in interior environs. These designs go beyond the building envelope, forming powerful sensory constructs, inspired by site-based opportunities.

The fifth chapter presents the ideas of Lisa Claypool, the Associate Professor of the History of Art, Design, and Visual Culture at the University of Alberta. Her chapter entitled 'Touring Spaceship Earth: A systems approach to teaching sustainable design in the remote classroom' poses the question: how to teach an introduction to the history of design, as well as the history of art and visual culture, that disrupts the normative geopolitics of first-year university students about the 'West' and the 'non-West?' Shifting from a content-based to a skills-based course (one that focuses on visual analysis and ways of seeing, for instance) is an obvious strategy. Remote course delivery offers another possibility: a weekly virtual tour of a museum or site across the planet that allows students to literally see things differently, to practice skills learned in asynchronous teaching videos during the week, and to bring home the relevance of the key questions driving each unit (for example, 'what is sustainable design?'). This chapter discusses object lessons from such pedagogical adventures across Spaceship Earth.

Each of these chapters and the book as a whole encourages us to reflect on site in the bigger picture of design education, drawing from the fields of art history, literature, philosophy, social and environmental justice, sociology, material studies, and visual culture. They offer examples that promote teachers and learners to think about site beyond the conventions of a physical place, considering it on different scales, in virtual environments, in hypothetical scenarios, or in different intellectual and social media. Effectively, each of the authors whose work is presented here brings up issues that point out opportunities for future research on different ways to advance the scholarship of site in design education.

Notes

1 Tina Richardson, *Walking Inside Out* (Lanham: Rowman & Littlefield, 2015); Jane Rendell, *Site-Writing: The Architecture of Art Criticism* (London: Bloomsbury Academic, 2010); Neil Spiller, *Visionary Architecture: Blueprints of the Modern Imagination* (London: Thames & Hudson, 2007); Grahame Shane, "The Emergence of Landcape Urbanism," in *The Landscape Urbanism Reader*, ed. Charles Waldheim (New York: Princeton Architectural Press, 2006); Georgia Daskalakis, Charles Waldheim, and Jason Young, eds., *Stalking Detroit* (London: Actar, 2001); Nathaniel Coleman, "The Myth of Autonomy,"

Architecture Philosophy 1, no. 2 (2015); David Harvey, *Spaces of Global Capitalism* (London: Verso, 2006); Pier Vittorio Aureli, *The Possibility of an Absolute Architecture* (Cambridge: MIT Press, 2011); Colin Rowe and Fred Koetter, *Collage City* (Cambridge: MIT, 1983); Marc Augé, *Non-Places: An Introduction to Supermodernity* (London: Verso, 2008); David Leatherbarrow, *Topographical Stories, Studies in Landscape and Architecture* (Philadelphia: University of Pennsylvania Press, 2004); Mark Smout, Laura Allen, *Augmented Landscapes* (New York: Princeton Architectural Press, 2007); Gevork Hartoonian, *The Crisis of the Object: The Architecture of Theatricality* (New York: Routledge, 2006); John Rajchman, *Constructions* (Cambridge: MIT Press, Constructions); Michael Hensel, *Grounds and Envelopes* (New York: Routledge, 2015); Kelly Shannon, "From Theory to Resistance: Landscape Urbanism in Europe," in *The Landscape Urbanism Reader*, ed. Charles Waldheim (Princeton Architectural Press, 2006); Yi-Fu Tuan, *Topophilia: a Study of Environmental Perception, Attitudes, and Values* (Englewood Cliffs: Prentice-Hall, 1974); Alan Colquhoun, "The Concept of Regionalism," in *Architectural Regionalism*, ed. Vincent B. Canizaro (New York: Princeton Architectural, 2007); Liane Lefaivre and Alexander Tzonis, *Critical Regionalism: Architecture and Identity in a Globalized World* (Munich: Prestel, 2003); Stan Allen, *Points and Lines: Diagrams and Projects for the City* (New York: Princeton Architectural Press, 1999); David Grahame Shane, *Recombinant Urbanism* (Sussex: Wiley-Academy, 2005).
2 Laura Sanderson and Sally Stone, *Emerging Practices in Architectural Pedagogy* (London: Routledge, 2021).
3 Kyna Leski, *Storm of Creativity* (Cambridge: MIT Press, 2020).
4 Genevieve S. Baudoin, *Interpreting Site: Studies in Perception, Representation, and Design* (London: Routledge, 2015).
5 Ilka Ruby and Andreas Ruby, *Groundscapes. The Re-Discovery of the Ground in Contemporary Architecture* (Barcelona: Gustavo Gili, 2006).
6 David Leatherbarrow, *Uncommon Ground: Architecture, Technology, and Topography* (Cambridge: MIT Press, 2000).
7 Michael Hensel and Christian Hermansen Cordua, *Constructions: An Experimental Approach to Intensely Local Architectures* (London: Wiley, 2015).
8 Malcolm Miles, *Urban Utopias* (London: Routledge, 2008); Robert Fishman, *Urban Utopias in the Twentieth Century* (New York: Basic Books, 1977); Stanley Buder, *Visionaries and Planners* (Oxford: Oxford University Press, 1990); Terence Riley, ed., *The Changing of the Avant-Garde* (New York: Museum of Modern Art, 2002); David Pinder, *Visions of the City* (Edinburgh: Edinburgh University Press, 2005).
9 Mark Wigley, "Whatever Happened to Total Design?," *Harvard Design Magazine* 5 (Summer 1998); Edward Saïd, *Orientalism* (London: Routledge, 1978); Dipesh Chakrabarty, *Provincializing Europe: Postcolonial Thought and Historical Difference* (Princeton: Princeton University Press, 2000); Kim Dovey, *Framing Places: Mediating Power in Built Form* (London: Routledge, 1999); Homi K. Bhabha, "Signs Taken for Wonders," ed. Bill Ascroft, Gareth Griffiths, and Helen Tiffin (London: Routledge).

Bibliography

Allen, Stan. *Points and Lines: Diagrams and Projects for the City*. New York: Princeton Architectural Press, 1999.
Augé, Marc. *Non-Places: An Introduction to Supermodernity*. London: Verso, 2008.
Aureli, Pier Vittorio. *The Possibility of an Absolute Architecture*. Cambridge: MIT Press, 2011.
Baudoin, Genevieve S. *Interpreting Site: Studies in Perception, Representation, and Design*. London: Routledge, 2015.
Bhabha, Homi K. *Signs Taken for Wonders*, edited by Bill Ascroft, Gareth Griffiths and Helen Tiffin, 29–36. London: Routledge.
Buder, Stanley. *Visionaries and Planners*. Oxford: Oxford University Press, 1990.
Chakrabarty, Dipesh. *Provincializing Europe: Postcolonial Thought and Historical Difference*. Princeton: Princeton University Press, 2000.
Coleman, Nathaniel. "The Myth of Autonomy." *Architecture Philosophy* 1, no. 2 (2015): 157–78.
Colquhoun, Alan. "The Concept of Regionalism." In *Architectural Regionalism*, edited by Vincent B. Canizaro, 147–55. New York: Princeton Architectural, 2007.
Daskalakis, Georgia, Charles Waldheim, and Jason Young, eds. *Stalking Detroit*. London: Actar, 2001.
Dovey, Kim. *Framing Places: Mediating Power in Built Form*. London: Routledge, 1999.
Fishman, Robert. *Urban Utopias in the Twentieth Century*. New York: Basic Books, 1977.
Hartoonian, Gevork. *The Crisis of the Object: The Architecture of Theatricality*. New York: Routledge, 2006.
Harvey, David. *Spaces of Global Capitalism*. London: Verso, 2006.
Hensel, Michael. *Grounds and Envelopes*. New York: Routledge, 2015.
Hensel, Michael, and Christian Hermansen Cordua. *Constructions: An Experimental Approach to Intensely Local Architectures*. London: Wiley, 2015.
Leatherbarrow, David. *Topographical Stories, Studies in Landscape and Architecture*. Philadelphia: University of Pennsylvania Press, 2004.
———. *Uncommon Ground: Architecture, Technology, and Topography*. Cambridge: MIT Press, 2000.
Lefaivre, Liane, and Alexander Tzonis. *Critical Regionalism: Architecture and Identity in a Globalized World*. Munich: Prestel, 2003.
Leski, Kyna. *Storm of Creativity*. Cambridge: MIT Press, 2020.
Miles, Malcolm. *Urban Utopias*. London: Routledge, 2008.
Pinder, David. *Visions of the City*. Edinburgh: Edinburgh University Press, 2005.
Rajchman, John. *Constructions*. Cambridge: MIT Press, Constructions.
Rendell, Jane. *Site-Writing: The Architecture of Art Criticism*. London: Bloomsbury Academic, 2010.

Richardson, Tina. *Walking Inside Out*. Lanham: Rowman & Littlefield, 2015.
Riley, Terence, ed. *The Changing of the Avant-Garde*. New York: Museum of Modern Art, 2002.
Rowe, Colin, and Fred Koetter. *Collage City*. Cambridge: MIT, 1983.
Ruby, Ilka, and Andreas Ruby. *Groundscapes. The Re-Discovery of the Ground in Contemporary Architecture*. Barcelona: Gustavo Gili, 2006.
Saïd, Edward. *Orientalism*. London: Routledge, 1978.
Sanderson, Laura, and Sally Stone. *Emerging Practices in Architectural Pedagogy*. London: Routledge, 2021.
Shane, David Grahame. *Recombinant Urbanism*. Sussex: Wiley-Academy, 2005.
Shane, Grahame. "The Emergence of Landcape Urbanism." In *The Landscape Urbanism Reader*, edited by Charles Waldheim, 56–68. New York: Princeton Architectural Press, 2006.
Shannon, Kelly. "From Theory to Resistance: Landscape Urbanism in Europe." In *The Landscape Urbanism Reader*, edited by Charles Waldheim, 141–62. New York: Princeton Architectural Press, 2006.
Smout, Mark, Laura Allen. *Augmented Landscapes*. New York: Princeton Architectural Press, 2007.
Spiller, Neil. *Visionary Architecture: Blueprints of the Modern Imagination*. London: Thames & Hudson, 2007.
Tuan, Yi-Fu. *Topophilia: A Study of Environmental Perception, Attitudes, and Values*. Englewood Cliffs: Prentice-Hall, 1974.
Wigley, Mark. "Whatever Happened to Total Design?". *Harvard Design Magazine* 5 (Summer 1998): 1–8.

1 Mutable Atmospheres
A Lens In to Look Out

Chelsea D. Limbird

Introduction

Can design begin with a memory? Can it originate in observation? Can the process for a proposed space that will be perceived by the senses commence with an immersion into sensory perception?

In an educational arc of spatial design, the pedagogy often focuses on a generative process established in a concept-based framework that directs the outcome. The result or consequence of these processes, as communicated through tools and techniques of design presentation, tends toward representations of experience in dialog with, and often intended as proposals for, physically constructed environments. These environments, made of materials, understood through the senses and translated to us through our own, visceral understanding of being in the world, intertwine lived and imagined paradigms. A project is, therefore, a married articulation of memories and a proposal for an imagined future that is yet to be.

To achieve the proposal, at its essence, a dream conveyed as a possible reality, or the design of an experience, is it possible to articulate a process of design that looks at and works through experience itself? If atmospheres of spatial experiences are defined by our sensory perception, understood through our memory and comprehended in a merging of presence and imagination, might we work within and through our observations and dreams to propose new environments and new atmospheres in which to live?

Can experience inform experience?
Can atmosphere be the beginning and serve as means to an end?
Can atmosphere be the project?

In this chapter, I will present these questions, as investigated by a group of students who came together to participate in a remote design studio workshop in the space and time of the summer of 2020, amid the initial months of the COVID-19 pandemic. The students ranged in their educational background and discipline, but collectively all had advanced past foundational or core years of at an undergraduate level of an art or design program. The framework of the traditional academic design studio is traditionally carried out and entrenched in the physical, constructed environment of the studio itself. Here, the collective energy of togetherness shifted to a remote, online classroom, spanned distance and, in many ways, stretched the members of the class to new understandings of intimacy and proximity. The students seemed to extend the time, listening to each word and each story, and, in a variety of different, unexpected ways, became closer in their solitude and through distance in their shared, elastic, circumstances, disparate histories and willingness to dream. Approaches to content, process and pedagogy shifted as the conversation changed from physical space of interaction and making to the space of the screen, a world both familiar and unfamiliar, a world requiring different recognition and communication of sense, empathy and understanding. The arc of investigations reflected individual isolation, space and time with voices of introspection and the possibility of identifying local and personally resonant sites for design intervention.

In addition, the online, screen-based classroom invited the use of time-based representation such as film, animation and video, to articulate and communicate spatial and sensorial ideas. This media offered a vehicle and a platform for the students to relate clearly developed studies of space, sequence and material as visceral experience. Simultaneously, this multilayered media invited revelations and disclosure of emotive secrets, hidden subtexts and whispered stories, between the lines and amid the frames. The students used time-based representation and sequential, sensorial narratives based in time as their primary tools in the design process and production. These temporal methodologies and frameworks invited and allowed seamless experimentation to presentation of experience of space. Atmospheres unfolded, in time, as sensorial experiences to be tested, understood, questioned and shared, in the process and as part of the conversation.

A Lens In

The structure of the studio required an initial laboratory-like study of the self. Individuals focused on attempting to understand the nature of personal perception of space, material and memory. The goal of the self-analysis aimed at appreciating oneself closely enough to find commonalities, elements shared or, in some cases, achieve a conversation of what this process allows and how it might invite a designer to proceed. In many ways, this initial investment and disclosure provided an open forum infused with empathetic understanding in the space of the studio. In a process of looking closely into their own spaces, lives, routines, rhythms, histories, cultures and landscapes, students began a search for an intimate, qualitative understanding of the character of the world in which they dwell. Narrative, as defined in association with each moment in the process, tied qualities of sense or esthetic indisputably to individual and a life or memory of place. These narratives, in many ways, not only defined the experience but also in essence were the experience and the memory. They could not be disassociated from the space and time of the senses that defined the atmosphere of the association with the memory. The experience in the world, in a site and associated with a situation, was the story it told and the one it continued to tell in the mind.

Self-study merged with spatial studies, while introspection heightened the conversation. Initial esthetic appreciation led to further studies questioning the interaction of body and space. Revelations of mind, memory, presence and dream intertwined to quality and account for these observed progressions.

Researching, documenting, questioning and representing these deeply personal, environmental and sensual atmospheres often encouraged students to shift, clarify and invent a lens that had initially offered a particular view of an experience. From a changed perspective or distance, the view became distorted, blurred or unrecognizable. Modes of inquiry suggested ways in which the methodology of the research itself might be applied to the techniques of communication and presentation in current and latter stages of the project as the story and the work itself required translation to others. In this way, the still photograph, written passage and even the static three-dimensional model, all lacked, most essentially, time. Narrative had become so deeply embedded in the work that the requisite element ground to a halt in most traditional representation. The students sought layered and fragmented means to convey and seek true paths to communicate their ideas. Experiments with representational strategies of collage, montage, animation, film, sound, performance and poetry intertwined and tested these conversions of sensory, space-time narratives in order to share and further understand as translations of experiences in the world.

In some ways, this research underlined and posed a question to the nature and definition of research itself as an element in the design process. Can memory be research? Can a story, recalled through the experience of a human sense, be research? Can associations between dreams and experience presented in sequenced sound and film narratives be research? Can this research inspire a process leading to a new understanding of experience? If the research, in essence, begins and grows in response to the body's sensory being in the world, might it derive a spatial experience finely tuned to this original instrument of study? Can our senses tell a story? Do our senses have a history? Can our senses be a site?

Collecting Atmospheres

In the beginning, students questioned relationships of time and distance by collecting, mapping and documenting the personal, individual spaces and sequences of the everyday. The body and mind dwelling in itself and in sites in the world served to anchor the initial research to place, location and perception. Observation and presence mediated through intimate sensory awareness and led to questions of documentation, translation, transformation and presentation. Here, "the lens in" doubled in meaning as it also informed the representational tools employed to communicate these catalogs of sensed realities, memories and dreams. Students, seeking appropriate means of communication and methodology of understanding, captured and presented their research and translations of spatial imagination through tools of time-based media, specifically techniques of film and stop-motion animation. Individuals derived unique methods and innovated languages through processes that revealed and communicated, both to themselves and to others, sensory, emotive and qualitative elements of space and time.

Representing Perception: Atmospheres of the Day

How do you remember the world? How do you remember a dream or a story? How do you recall a color or a place? If the initial research underlined, most often, the visualizations of memories, accumulations of perceived senses and the stories our mind intertwine with those collections of past experiences, the students needed means, techniques and methods in order to produce and share these discoveries. The collections of atmospheres ranged by individual and even singular student studies and perceptions varied widely. Consistently, visuals linked to words, expounding narrated worlds, seemingly unbound by the limits of language. It seemed the research, initiated through a sensory perception or memory of that sensory experience, had unlocked and freed a caged and spirited tale. This was a language we all shared. Initial photographs, short films with sound and original works created in response to an emotion, mood or quality of space, all pointed to discussions of time and sequence. Questions of distance, depth, temperature, texture, balance, gravity, strength or tension, all became as pressing and meaningful as inquiries into the appropriate means to convey patience, homesickness, loneliness, exuberance or joy. A moment of silence in a presentation or fading black at the end of a classmate's film held our breath like white space on the page. The translations from individual memory and experience to auditory-visual time-based presentation, infused with emotion and narrative, were each diverse and didactic. Each represented not only an investment of time and energy, but also trust in oneself as an individual and in the shared experience of the group. These criteria further underlined a collective confidence and spirit in the process of the design studio and in the discursive frameworks of the ideas and the project as a whole.

Because of the advanced level and experience of the students in the studio, no specific requirements of media or format were given in assigning the initial collection of atmospheres. In many ways, the open format in this beginning research and presentation also served as an informal measure of the range and capacity of the class, a group of students amassed from a range of disciplines and academic programs. In parallel to this, the open format allowed each student to seek out, develop and establish her own representational language in the project as a whole. An initial presentation of a combination of slides and film clips that included fine art, found objects, photography, landscapes, portraits, color plates and material studies, interior architecture and other intimate and personal moments specific to the instructor's own life was accompanied by a semi-autobiographic narrative, relating a sensorial translation and deeper meaning of the visuals. Essentially, this presentation offered a lens into a landscape of a narrated set of memories, loosely connected and personally curated. This immediately offered a model for the students, not in a precise or definite answer, but a way to consider a possible process of reflection, collection and presentation. In another way, the instructor had taken the first risk in front of the group, dissecting and uncovering her own sensory experience of the world and, in a way, giving everyone permission to do the same.

In some projects, students recreated an image or experience through a process of making. These representations translated the mood of activity and perception into composition, color, line and, often, collaged assemblies of material. With interpretation, students further observed memory, distilled, interpreted and iteratively transformed their initial visualizations. One student recounted the childhood smell of green pea paste after the rain on a playground with an exaggerated forest of various shades of green water colored onto a clean white background, the deeper greens soaking over the lighter, translucent green-yellow below. The bean paste painting is presented beside a photograph at night, almost completely black. The single light in the middle in the lower third of the image reveals in the distance, the playground, now, only a shadow to walk by after dark on the way home. The eye lingers on the distant light and an eclipsed memory of another time. A second atmosphere and narrative shared by the same student passes through a grain distillery and while the green watercolor layered forest returns in form, now a dry field of tan and brown desiccates this memory's season and air. The edges of each color field seem almost golden ochre and lift away from the space of the page as parting words at the end of a day. The accompanying photograph reveals a house, deep in these tanned trees. All seemed to be wearing the same colors of gold, yellow and brown; even the sky is warm white-yellow and dry. It was a sepia tone photograph, found in a drawer or left, for years, in the pages of a book, drying in the sun. A memory of old popsicles assumed the faded blues and greens of their plastic cases, dreamed together, reflecting in the fluorescent light of the neighborhood convenience store. An old friend's room glowed light yellow and white edges of lace, dancing light and whispers, shadows and secrets. Childhood activities like playing in the snow transformed into a motion of the heart, a rhythm of limbs, undeniably known and, at once, stored and fading away. This memory, along with the others in this list, was transcribed graphically in an effort to communicate a combined sense of emotion and youth, playfulness and joy with a staccato of carefree energy cast through the marks made on the two-dimensional surface of the page. The final layer communicating these worlds was the voice of the student when she shared the drawing and paired photograph with the class, a voice unfolding memories now part of the shared experience of the project.

Often, when a student presented a collection of atmospheres with parallel images, photographs and drawings or paintings, the side-by-side, still images of the memory, would inspire dialog within the studio. An exquisite corpse-like conversation would ensue as a result of the random, and often deep-seated, associations others would make with an image, color, texture or sensory environment. In some instances, these translations extracted particular qualities of light and atmosphere. They appealed to the senses and to a collectively shared perception of space, material, season or time of day. Certain textures conjured material realities while particular color relationships spoke, most consistently to weather and temperature associated with moments in the calendar year. In other work, the making of marks evoked psychological and mental stresses reminiscent of situations and emotional weight brought on by myriad forces of life from family and health to structures of education and the pressure and question of success. In some of the projects, the presence and passage of time persisted through the narratives of images and the abstractions told more than the words. Questions of aging, responsibility and the divisions and boundaries between adulthood and childhood pressed and crept through a quiet grayness in the representation. The space of a trampoline presented in a series of drawings expressed the rhythm of jumping, moments of contact and the feelings of weightlessness. The image gathered the cadence and candor of a beating heart with the poise and balance of balloons slowly disappearing in the air. Color further defined and energized the work, articulating something between joy and fear, leaving the unanswered questions, still and suspended, in the sky. Together we witnessed, in the presentations, each student revisiting a site and reliving a unique situation and in the representation of this work, through the telling of these stories and the creation of the imagination of the images, at that moment, we shared something new in the present.

Some students located and represented atmospheres by comparing distinct places they were aware of at different moments in their lives. Emotional attachments to these places, their inhabitants and local customs contrasted the notion of formal unity within political and geographic boundaries. The narrative extended further, telling a story of movement and passage in space. Shifting notions of life's early foundations and perceptions landscape changes, drastically and dramatically, in a short period of time became key to a story told through the shifting tactility of material fibers. The narrative became coherent in the presentation with deep contrast, translucent met opaque and different homes known in the same country defined the same person had to split a life into two. Students questioned, through the work, whether one might recognize the self across the map of a country with cultures as disparate and diverse as its land and geography. These inquiries persisted through layers of images of weather and textures of fading landscapes and sky. The work created a sensorial language that resounded and communicated this story of time, distance, home and disillusion, through languages of humidity, barometric pressure and cycles of seasons and moments in the year.

In the project of collecting atmospheres, a productive and revelatory path through the analysis and synthesis looked more deeply at an experience as a whole, considered its parts and pieces to, then, reconfigure it in order to uncover and reveal something new, unexpected and previously untold. In a way, the experience would begin in pieces and scattered like a puzzle and, through the process of connecting senses perceived to these fragments of memory, the representation of the atmosphere would link, form and come together. An example of this method for working through the process can be traced through the work of a student who recalled the extreme disorientation she experienced upon exiting an underground metro station in an unfamiliar neighborhood in Beijing. She described a dream-like unsteadiness that left her feeling as through she no longer stood on solid ground or, in fact, that she was still and the ground was moving below her. In the representation, color and material layered into a dense, low-relief collage to express a clouded reflection and a dizzying, kaleidoscopic sense of space. Movement blurred brightness and transparent geometries danced in tandem with irregular lines weaving through a composition marrying surreal visions with a clarity of daylight and keen, almost overwhelming, awareness of physical surroundings. A classmate noted the irony of this presentation of a particular emotion, familiar to many in the group in a variety of situations the student had clearly presented the feeling of being lost, an emotional state of feeling without or empty, with an abundance of constructed material and a mass of words. The inertia of the memory of being lost, in the process of remembering and synthesizing the pieces of the experience, had inverted this emptiness into accumulation and matter. It invited a new tactile sense of the experience in as a fullness of its occurrence and an evolved reflection on its memory.

In a similar approach to the project, a second atmosphere by the same student conveyed the sensory experience of her movement through the city, a pedestrian among vehicles, in and out of light, under concrete highways overhead, beside and among every sound of urban life. Both knowing a path taken and a destination, the body was free to absorb the cacophony of the space for all of its symphonies of endless engines, murmurings of moving air and echoing caverns of paved and tunneled surfaces. Beyond this, color and smell and sense without name or origin captivated and drew the walking figure forward on her path. Understanding distance as a point of view, the perspective was framed and arched by the constructs of the auditory

Figure 1.1 "Atmospheres of the Day, The story of underpasses and viaducts" by Jing Wang.

environment holding the body while structuring and composing the space (Figure 1.1). The strength and value in this process was the beginning observation and documentation in the site in the everyday, as a pedestrian, in an urban environment, that led to the translation of a series of collectively understood narratives, interwoven into the fabric of a quilt-like tapestry of spatial and sensory experience. The student sought solace and a type of moving meditation in these daily walks through seemingly singular looping, weaving lines of light gray highway shrouded by black shadows, revealing acute triangles of blue sky. She imagined the intermittent siren in red and a distant, indiscernible voice in transparent, lemon yellow. A transformation of her ritualized path carved as a thin black line, tied around itself made the day only knot her world together, casting it into a dream of a single iconic image, framed in the composition of the two-dimensional page. Seeking, reflecting, transforming and sharing grounded the proposals and shaped the practice of the larger project. These initial studies and conversations of atmosphere, very often immediately from the present day, set up the practice of observation and meditations in space to be carried through the arc of the studio work.

Atmospheres in Time

In the next iteration of the work, time-based representation opened a variety of potential experiential, psychological and sensorial understandings communicated through the layers of the narratives. Students tested sequence, duration, distance, sound and a range of production techniques to present the atmospheres that had been previously fixed or captured in a moment in time. Weaving together initial imagery with narrative underlined, in most cases, an addition of another sense of perception in experience. Sound recordings in space and musical scores attempting to accentuate or parallel a particular emotive quality in the work became a key figure in production. The work itself ranged greatly from content to technique, often a reflection of the original atmosphere collection and resulting conversation or, in some cases, a tangential inspiration from the story being told. In some cases, a student's particular facility with the media led to the technique in a project or the production of the work resulted from an experiment with the media itself. Examples included a fragmented look into the everyday of an urban landscape becoming a layered montage of a city's jungle origins and its concrete future, accompanying by a looping instrumental beat, all relating the story of contemporary development and planning in one student's city. The endless construction seemed to be building the same site into infinity, the phenomenon kept in line with the soundtrack to his repeating clip. Another student linked together a series of clips of famous Hollywood films in order to present her own mood and experience. She interspersed these film clips with a video of herself, painting a watercolor describing her day like a timeline of color and form. As a final layer, her voice spoke a story describing her theory of the day, the range of moods and emotions each person moves through in a single twenty-four hour period, describing just one day to be almost like a lifetime of emotions. The words, as she spoke them, were also cast on the screen to be read by the viewer.

In another presentation of atmospheres in time, self-observation in isolation became the subject and content of a time-based narrative with psychological and introspective clues established through more advanced film editing tools. The film portrayed a single shot view into a studio apartment with its occupant, the student, going through a single day in isolation, unable to leave and without much focus or motivation to do more than get through the day, singular meaningless activities are each skimmed through in dream-like slow motion in a media quality reminiscent of the visual grain and deep contrast of early silent film. The ticking of a clock, the sound of an alarm, chirping birds from an open window and the endless drone of a radio newscast turned down low pervaded the vision of this pandemic reality, a banal truth of an interior encountering the self and the self alone. Layers of random geometric or seemingly filmic visions overtake the screen intermittently and visual stimuli would divert the viewer for distracted intervals of hallucinations or daydream-like asides. Moments of diverted attention only deepen the concentrated ennui of the room and our palpable empathy for the protagonist. These diverse projects bridged cityscape with an eternal construction site, lived realities finding themselves in parallel with the fictitious lives and scenes in Hollywood film and proposed the interior space of our home as a self-portrait revealing deep into the psyche. Each personified space and site while objectifying occupant, unifying the viewer and lending insight into our shared experience.

In another exploration, a student used material and the process of making to approach a metaphor where a series of experiments in three-dimensional craft formed, deconstructed and reformed an abstract body. The action conjured the structure, weight and shifting imbalance of situations and emotions. Posture took on and enveloped an atmosphere. Material, in its manipulation, recounted memory.

These initial film and time-based studies served as vehicles both to test the deployment of emergent media strategies and to provoke conversation through a shift in the form of representation as a proposal for a language of storytelling through the next steps of the process. The potential for deep layering of the sensory experience beyond the visual opened avenues for the communication of site, space, material and experience outside of the focus of ocular-centric conventions.

Adaptation Studies

The studio focus turned inside out for a moment, shifting away from the introspective, self-study to a period of case-study research. Continuing the thesis of the studio, the students questioned the possibilities of space and site as caverns of memory, full of stories and abundant with atmospheric qualities. Chosen specifically for narratives marked by edition or alteration, the students researched selected sites of adaptive reuse for the case studies, looking deeper into the historical, cultural and geographic context in each project. For each of the research and analysis studies, the focus varied both with the student and the case study itself. The diverse range of sites, designers, programs, histories, material approaches and embodied culture of each project lent rich ground for direction in the research, in-class conversation and shared associations between existing, built work and the ideas and dialog already building and being shared in the studio itself. Students found conceptual foundations and design processes in the archives of representation and documentation of each project. In many cases, they also gained an understanding of the translation of the notions of memory of culture and place through time as spatial and sensory experience of a project, underlining and further emphasizing the beginning work in the studio sequence and drawing attention to the possibility of looking to observation, atmosphere and presence as design tools and methodologies.

In the process, pairs of students were assigned a case study, each to undertake their own research, analysis and presentation to the studio, but linked in order to foster a dialog and, potentially, debate inspired from different points of view. In all cases, students were researching at a distance from the physical and geographical sites of the case studies, attempting to gather experiential understanding as a full story of the space, and, in the end, share and convey this information coherently and succinctly, in our own remote setting, to their peers. These multiple distances of information exchange and communication interplay were not new to the group who had been entrenched in the reality of the pandemic for a little over half of a year. Still, the questions of the studio brought many lingering questions to the forefront of the conversation. How can experience of place be shared at a distance? How can sensory perception, understood wholly by the body, in the space of a physically constructed site, be understood through representation? What media communicates this? Do the translations of each of our own understandings of the world speak clearly? Is there something lost when we are attempting to recreate and retell experience? Is there something in the moments of experience itself that can never truly be represented? These questions further emphasized the space that the studio occupied in the educational arc of the students as well as in the place and time in the context of the world. When faced with questions of communicating ideas of space as an experience, how can these ideas be shared?

Within the research, essential questions grounded relationships between programmatic use and conditions of atmospheric qualities before and after an adaptation of a constructed space. The case study analysis work spanned diverse location, program and design approach, all linked conceptually with the shared characteristic of mutability, an attribute defined most clearly through a history of change and, in many instances, a total eclipse of previous use to assume a new identity or form. The tenet of mutability became a key component of the conversation in the research. It pointed to questions of design intention in a site with an existing structure that holds a memory of history, society and culture within its spaces, material and skeleton of its body. Adaptive reuse and this idea of mutability celebrate site as an enduring document of life and generational evolution. Looking for the elements that have lasted through time and understanding the fragments that persist through renovation and preservation, weather and time itself, cast a deep lens into ideas of sustainability through layers of ecology, environment and material to histories of bureaucracy, politics and economics. The powerful revelation that the site brings a considerable list of requirements to achieve what many were defining as "sustainable" gleaned some shock from many of the students in the process.

Within the research, students collected images, drawings and texts in order to relate stories, across time, of mutation and mutability. The work, thereby, sought to derive a visual anthology of important touchstones for a codified approach to representation. Definitions of atmosphere intertwined conceptually and experientially with understandings of space, material, detail and sequence. The research opened and evolved perspectives into ideas of spaces understood simultaneously and coherently with the senses and inside the mind (Figure 1.2).

The research incorporated the scale of surrounding neighborhood and the density of the existing landscape. It shifted to the scale of the body, occupation, and asked what a body can do, how it interacts and how it encounters the world. Questions investigated adaptation

Figure 1.2 "Adaptation Case Study, Storefront for Art and Architecture, Concept and Experience" by Xueni Hu.

Mutable Atmospheres 23

as a gesture of the built environment and as an understanding of the in-between: between space and time, between people, between uses, between the mutable lapses and between atmospheres.

With two students focused on each assigned case study, dialog ensued and each presented a variety of points of view and insights about the work. In researching the University Metro Station in Naples, Italy, one student focused on the surfaces and textures of the city. Another looked more closely at social influences and atmospheres of inhabitation, delving into urban spaces immediately related to the project. In further research in the metro station investigating human occupation and the scale of the body in the space, questions focused on point of view, vision as corporeal experience and access understood through the vertical section. The section indicated and defined through varying ceiling heights associated with programmatic requirements and the experience within the interior sliced through the project in direct dialog with a highly graphic interior facades accompanying the path of vertical circulation and the visual experience of visitors ascending and descending escalators and stairs. In dialog with this section drawing, another student's vertical cut analysis of the Metro Station revealed the layered, chromatic chaos of the project in a perspectival section that unfolds as one descends through subterranean levels toward reaching the train platform (Figure 1.3).

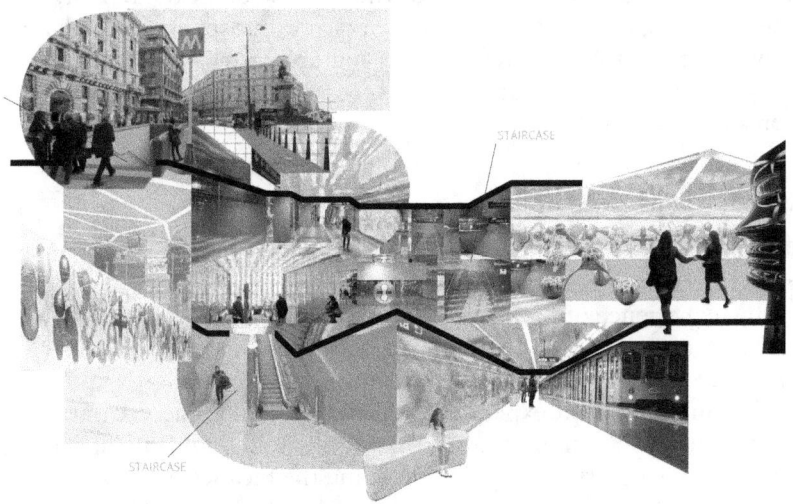

Figure 1.3 "Adaptation Case Study, University Metro Station, Site Section" by Yanya Mei.

24 Chelsea D. Limbird

The case studies in adaptive reuse provided a foundation for understanding the potential evolution of emptiness in the spaces forgotten or left behind in the wake of changing circumstances. In studying and observing parallel projects, students discovered and defined ideas of mutable spaces, silence and the capacity to reconsider and reimagine form, use, material and atmosphere through site, scale and the senses. Personal and historical narratives strengthened the work and allowed the students to understand potentials outside of the case studies, for other sites and for applications in other spaces and other times.

Mutable Sites

In translating the largely autobiographical, atmospheric work and case study findings into foundational underpinnings for design proposals, students first reflected on the events of the early months of the pandemic. What had they witnessed? The students investigated personal and shared changes and tectonic shifts in the cultural, economic and social landscapes of their lives. Adding to these investigations, students examined alterations in routine in concert with modified or altered scenes and atmospheres within the built environment of their local cities and towns, the homes where so much that had been stable and familiar had changed quickly and become different and unfamiliar. Continuing, they interrogated and attempted to define the concept of mutability and mutable space within these contexts and environments. In this process, the frameworks of atmosphere and adaptive reuse intertwined sites identified as mutable, carrying forward each project through the imaginative spectra of time, experience and sensory perception.

Sensory Upgrade

For one student, recent municipal mandates for signage that homogenized particular neighborhoods had erased the character and joy out of the experience of the street. The student identified a specific artery of her own neighborhood and proposed color as a tool for constructing a sense of place, ultimately attempting to infuse energy and inspiration into the lived experiences of everyday life. She dreamed of a vibrant urban community, a site that would hold forever in one's memory with the colors of graphics adorning the facades like open invitations with charm and beauty. She imagined a brilliant night landscape of lights filled with energy and ensuring safety due to the continuous activity and presence of friends and businesses along the illuminated

Figure 1.4 "Mutable Sites, Sensory Upgrade, Before/After Collage" by Savannah Shi.

path. Her intention underlined an escape from homogeneity, a world where every street had become an endless, unvarying recurrence of the same façade. Instead, she envisioned a place enriched and radiating difference and embracing community, filled with life, activity, culture and conversation (Figure 1.4). She communicated this through an animation that began empty and quiet and slowly gathered and gained energy, sound and color. It layered with chromatic fields, light and a rhythm of upbeat sounds, shifting its scene from day to night and relaying a cadence and candor of urban joy, twenty-four hours across the facades of the street.

The Boundary Compound

Examining local sites and their degraded ecologies due to industrialization and modernization, one student looked specifically at the relationships between the recent trends in the lives and habitats of birds in relationship to airports and airfields in China. She identified and isolated one particular airport where bird populations posed a significant problem for the flight patterns of the planes. She collected and analyzed data on the likelihood that birds would encounter planes in flight within a given range of the horizontal plan of the airfield.

Considering the mental and physical trauma of these encounters on both birds and humans, her proposal to adapt the space of the airfield repositions the emotional impacts a bird might feel when struck by a plane as the catalyst to choreograph the human experience within a museum. Both form and atmosphere incorporated disorientation, imbalance and isolation. Throughout the space of the museum, the human, metaphorically experiencing the bird's encounter with a plane, lacks a clear line of site and is, in a way, incapacitated, unable to walk a straight path to the final destination. Formally composed of a wall reaching to the sky and a low-lying building for the museum itself, the project alters the takeoff and landing patterns of the planes as well as the flight patterns of the species of birds most affected by the site of the airport.

The atmosphere within the museum catalogs the research and premise of the proposal while simultaneously preserving and presenting an unforgettable experience so it is ingrained in the memory, forsaken with a nightmarish quality. The student produced a film that captured the experience of the proposal, remarkably translating the feeling of disorientation, abstraction and fear with a loss of equilibrium into the space of an animated narrative, all set to a haunting score.

Interstellar Cinema

Through questions of distance and the nostalgic celebration of spaces to "go to the movies," a student conflated the intimacy of screening a film with the open air of a community garden as a paired program for adaptive reuse. Both spaces shared the unfortunate character of, at one time, knowing fervent activity but being left in limbo during times of quarantine. The space of the garden provided different and diverse points of view as a theatrical analogy to the spectacle of the cinema. Most importantly, the garden as a site provided enough space and air to remain open despite distancing requirements and potential, unforeseen, future restrictions and codes. As viewers remained paradoxically separated and, in the same moment, connected through collective viewing of the film, the familiarity of light and material offered some semblance of a previous existence and shared experience.

We are brought together by the story and by a new narrative to share, interwoven with memories and storylines of days and earlier films and some nostalgia for what we had. Her proposal for the spaces, presented as a film, represented these ideas through a sequential montage; a visitor promenades through the space of the proposed garden-cinema encountering archival footage of Charlie Chaplin in

"Modern Times" along this procession. In effect, the viewer is carried through the cinema experience interwoven, almost floating, through the reality of the space and the sequence of the film that they would be watching. The promenade of movement performs like a film, slowing down, speeding up and, at times, comes to a pause. Views into the space of the garden revealed a series of globe-like glass orbs for individual seating and viewing into the projected film. Like a futuristic landscape, the crystal spheres promise air and space for each visitor as well as a shiny surface for countless reflections to bounce off and play into the interior of the cinema-garden. The project performs and represents the gathering of atmospheres and communicates the experience of poignant memories in both its momentous present and in its fleeting passing.

Conclusion

The work only begins to open the possibilities of studying and employing atmosphere as elemental in the process of designing space. In many ways, the students recollected and searched through memories and situations of sites they had known in their lives in order to seek out a new site and imagine a new situation. There may have been something familiar, some sense or quality, the scale or the light and the shadows at a certain time of day that drew a student to a site to begin something new. It may have been a voice or a sound that she heard when passing or simply the way the place conjured the memory of another time, a dream indescribable in words. This served as a rich beginning to a design pedagogy that carried through the work and continuously strengthened the projects throughout the process.

Investigating the role of time-based media as integral to the process of a spatial design project, as it carried and supported narrative construction and communication of sensory perception and sequential experience, scaffolded the work throughout and opened a clear means of conversation between the students and the content of their ideas. Because the students used time in each step of the process, they were continuously thinking in the narrative entanglements of space. In constant dialog with stories and lived experience, their proposals centered interactivity, movement and sensory immersion. The communication of atmospheres and the design of atmospheres emerged in simultaneous production. In a sense, the atmosphere was the presentation and the project. It was the process of exploration and the product itself. There was no moment that indicated "the beginning of the final production." The arc of the course was calibrated by the arc of each author's thinking and, in its best form, became descriptive of an evolving arc of understanding.

We began with our senses, remembering place, sites, from experiences stored in our memory. In distilling these memories, attempting to understand the atmosphere of space, we were able to project these experiences forward into dreams of new situations and new narratives. In time, these proposals, projects and conversations grow and they, too, are stored and become part of our shared memory.

Bibliography

Albers, Josef. *The Interaction of Color*. New Haven: Yale University Press, 1975.
Benjamin, Walter. *Illuminations*. New York: Schocken Books, 1969.
Berger, Jon. *Ways of Seeing*. London: Penguin Books, 1973.
De Certeau, Michel. *The Practice of Everyday Life*. Berkeley: University of California Press, 2002.
Debord, Guy. *The Society of Spectacle*. New York: Zone Books, 1994.
Didion, Joan. *The White Album*. New York: Simon and Schuster, 1979.
Kertesz, Andre. *Andre Kertesz: Sixty Years of Photography*. New York: Penguin Books, 1978.
Marker, Chris, dir. *San Soleil*. 1983. Irvington: Criterion/Argos Films, 2007, film.
Pallasmaa, Juhani. *The Eyes of the Skin: Architecture and the Senses*. West Sussex: Wiley, 2012.
Perez-Gomez, Alberto. *Attunement*. Cambridge: MIT Press, 2016.
Rossi, Aldo. *Aldo Rossi, Projects and Drawings, 1962–1979*. New York: Rizzoli, 1979.
Sendak, Maurice. *In the Night Kitchen*. New York: Harper and Row, 1970.
Tschumi, Bernard. *The Manhattan Transcripts*. London: Academy Editions, 1994.
Tufte, Edward. *Envisioning Information*. Cheshire: Graphics Press, 1990.
Zumthor, Peter. *Atmospheres: Architectural Environments, Surrounding Objects*. Basel: Birkhäuser, 2006.

2 Going to Places and Staying at Home

Reflections on Critical Cartography and Desktop Documentation in Online Education

*Emily Bereskin and
Natacha Quintero González*

Introduction

First-hand observation and analysis of a particular site is an indisputable element of architectural and urban planning education as well as routine professional practice. At the beginning of any project, students conduct site-visits to familiarise themselves with the task at hand. They study the formal aspects of a space, its usage, scale, and context. Students are told to sit, observe, walk, run through a space— sometimes as teachers, we ask them walk backwards or skip—in order to appreciate different experiences of the area in question. They sketch, take photos, and record videos, so that when they are off-site, they have documentation of the locale at hand. These methods help students understand conditions not apparent in pictures, plans, and other visual representations, and develop their own ways of sensing and experiencing place.

Online education troubles this quintessential exercise, as students have no shared site they can access, particularly if the participants are scattered geographically. Within the purview of online teaching, then, how do we recreate this vital aspect of planning education? In this chapter, we call for a redesign of site-led research and design pedagogy based on recent scholarship in the fields of critical urban studies and relational theory that have helped reconceptualise the city (and all specific points within it) away from its Cartesian understanding and towards a conception of geographical sites as nodes, or loci along larger assemblages, which include not only material constructions, but also ecological systems, socio-political context, flows, and so on.[1]

DOI: 10.4324/9781003322726-3

In this chapter, we advocate for course design that considers site following such a conceptualisation of space, one which links everyday practices in the home with spatial processes happening *elsewhere*. We argue that such a focus enables students to not only rethink the definition of 'site', but also to engage with assignments which directly question the epistemology of digital learning, research, and presentation. We discuss three pedagogical strategies/techniques that link the students among home, city, region, and world, and that aid students in reflecting critically on online/real world differentiation throughout all steps of any course process: research, analysis, brainstorming, design, implementation, and communication.[2] First, we discuss the choice of a thematic focus which links home with global planning networks. Second, we examine the application of the 'follow-the-thing' research method to the online teaching context. Finally, we analyse the use of the desktop documentary as a self-reflexive presentation method for online research.

These strategies were developed as part of a teaching module held in the summer semester of 2020, within the context of the COVID-19 pandemic. The modules, which consisted of both a planning seminar and a master studio, were designed with experimental online formats as alternatives to traditional place-bound approaches. During the pandemic, online education was not a choice, but rather a necessity—and for many, a burden. Our students were scattered: stuck at home, in the middle of various towns and cities, but linked across international borders through networks of digital infrastructures and by numerous shared experiences despite geographical specificity. The course focus was therefore placed on this precise spatial reality in order to help students understand that cities are not spatial containers, but centres of global resource flows and emissions, and that their homes—no matter where they are found are part of this network.[3]

Approaching Sites Relationally

In conducting spatial analyses, planners typically avoid examining the city merely as a set of physical structures or considering only the causal factors for spatial phenomena. Instead, a spatial analysis looks at both the interactions of different effects within the city as well as their spatial implications.[4] Urban studies, and in particular recent research in geography and sociology, have shown that sites do not exist as bubbles, separate and independent from other points in cities or elsewhere in the world.[5] This idea draws on a relational understanding of urban space as a sum of multiple spatial networks and as places of nodal connectivity.[6] Sites, urban and otherwise, are seen less as confined spatial entities and more as embedded in global networks of economic, social, or political linkages.[7] Colin McFarlane argues that sites are spaces of *translocal relations*, drawing attention to the various forms of exchange, histories, materiality, labour, and power influences involved in their production and reproduction, characterising sites as performative and always in the making.[8] Adopting a relational perspective on the material and social production of sites means seeing the local and the global as co-constituted, and cities as sites within larger geographic spaces.[9] To appreciate such relationality, we only need to look at the increasing flow of urban resources—goods, capital, labour, information, or raw materials, moving in and across cities and connecting dispersed sites around the world through organised structures.[10]

Beyond material flows, urban sites, regardless of their size and composition, are also linked by networks of information, influence, organisation, political mobilisations, and technologies that ultimately blur the meaning of distance.[11] These features open up a way to understand sites beyond the physical realm to that which is *digital/virtual*, as they are increasingly constituted by the information recorded about them, whether in the form of detailed analyses produced by geographic information systems (GIS);[12] or through the attributes or meanings of place constructed through media.[13] Thanks to webs of physical and virtual infrastructures, we can *be* anywhere with just one click.

In the framework of our two courses, we, the authors and teachers of the course, considered sites as spatial units of analysis that can anchor global phenomena locally regardless of their size.[14] We purposefully included the home as a site of relations inseparable from global processes and nature.[15] Here, there exists a space where social—and societal—relationships are produced and reproduced. Examinations of inner architectures and spatial arrangements, the organisation of housework, or dwelling and consumption patterns are also integral aspects of urban planning and an urban planning education.[16] An understanding of the home as a relational site helped students link familiar everyday activities with broader scales and juxtapose different narratives circulating in physical and digital spaces in an effort to understand seemingly inaccessible systems.

Choice of Thematic Focus

An alternative to the spatially fixed site is thus a thematic focus that highlights the embeddedness of sites and cities in translocal networks. Given the global connectedness of nearly all aspects of our lives, one can imagine countless possibilities: waste, water, oil, textiles, nearly any resource or commodity. We, the teachers, chose to work with food, one of the most fundamental elements of human life and civilisation. As Dani Burrows argues, food grounds us in our most urgent contemporary issues and serves as an accessible gateway that allows us to question our ways of living.[17] From the very first human settlements, cities have been organised around the production, distribution, consumption, and disposal of food.[18] This gigantic effort has arguably the greatest social and physical impact on Earth, and yet, numerous processes behind it remain hidden.[19] How might food provide a link from home to urban planning processes, both local and global?

The seminar, 'Feeding the City', focused on mapping and researching the current state of complex food supply chains, while the master's studio, 'From the Region', required students to focus their attention on a specific case study in order to identify problems and propose interventions into a local food system. Unable to go anywhere together in person, the class began with a visit to home. The kitchen, where food is stored, prepared, and eaten, is often considered to be the centre and symbolic heart of the home. Its placement and design are fundamental to domestic architecture and settlement patterns,[20] and are an ideal place to begin when examining the relationship between food and spatial production. Visiting the home also underlines that we are not external components to food systems, but very much an integral part of them. To begin the semester, students were asked to document the preparation and consumption of a meal. In doing so, they were asked to consider the origin of the many individual ingredients, how those ingredients came to their kitchen, the tools and steps they used for cooking, the energy sources involved in processing, and the social dimension of the meal and its preparation. Students documented this exercise using a variety of formats and techniques including video-montage, stop-motion, and narrated videos, examining the commonly unattended aspects related to the purchase, cooking, consumption, and disposal of food and thereby situating themselves as active participants in food systems.

Following the Food Cycle from Home

Food preparation and eating may be a familiar part of our everyday lives; however, our routines are only a small part of a complex network of numerous—and often—processes that constitute the global food system. For the seminar 'Feeding the City', students examined these processes by first cataloguing and analysing all the stations of the food cycle from production sites to their homes and then by tracing individual food products from their pantries along the food supply chain itself. The students used a mapping methodology developed in order to represent built environments within commodity chains, the multiple scales involved in global food circuits, and the networks of actors that interact among these localities.[21] The idea of tracing products back to their origins was inspired by 'follow-the-thing' research approaches, which trace commodities through various sites to expose the connections among the production, trade, retail, consumption and disposal of goods.[22] Initially characterised by ethnographic analysis, 'follow-the-thing' work has evolved into an approach that is not methodologically rigid, and instead benefits from creative formats ranging from documentaries, to journal articles, to art installations.[23] By following seemingly trivial items, such as papayas, tomatoes, and broccoli, researchers show the advantages of multi-sited research in showing deeply entangled relationships between seemingly disconnected processes, as well as with the troubling realities behind global trade.[24] Not always having a coherent overarching narrative, 'follow-the-thing' studies engage audiences through accessible, simple vocabularies and descriptions of familiar situations. Yet, these stories emerge alongside new insights and often elicit critical thinking on moral and ethical issues related to global supply chains.

To set the framework, student groups were first tasked with designing and leading a seminar session focused on one station of the food cycle. Inspired by Carolyn Steel's *Hungry City: How Food Shapes Our Lives*, sessions were divided into the following: agricultural land, urban agriculture, factory, transport, market, online retail, public food-settings, the kitchen, the table, and the bin.[25] Students were asked to consider the historical development of the station, its spatial characteristics, and any current trends regarding operational issues or socio-ecological impacts. They were given freedom to use any available research materials, from scientific texts and exemplary projects to websites and other digital resources. Formats included a mixture of inputs with live interviews, moderation of guest speakers, interactive surveys, photo essays, text analyses, video/film analyses, and the use of the collaborative tools to draw maps and collectively brainstorm in the digital classroom.

Students examined the stations not only as sites of resource circulation, but also as spaces marked by multiple histories, unique sets of power relations, and complex social and environmental dynamics. Three themes dominated the discussions: (1) innovation and spatial change; (2) class and gender relations; and (3) cooking and collective activism. The first topic arose primarily in the discussion of transportation and food retail. Students mapped detailed insights into the complexities of logistics, including the role of technological innovation in maintaining efficiency and sustainability, and how these operations shape urban and industrial sites along with the infrastructures that connect them. At the following station, they then analysed the history of the market as a physical site, as well as the implications of the increasing digitalisation of food retail on its architectures and presence in the city. Another group analysed the use of architecture in efforts to increase transparency and ethical production in the meat industry. Discussions about class and gender relations developed primarily out of the groups focused on production sites, food factories, and the kitchen. One group concerned themselves with the relationship between the banana production and trade and food sovereignty movements in Ecuador, ultimately showing how neoliberal policies affect local economies and give rise to social mobilisations.[26] The group dedicated to 'the kitchen' presented a brief genealogical analysis looking at how different historical periods, technological development, and socio-cultural viewpoints about women have shaped this important space in the household over time. Finally, of particular significance was the repeated observation, across numerous settings, that collective practice of cooking can serve as a catalyst for political participation and transformative change.[27] Concrete examples were given by a group focusing on place-settings for cooking and eating in public and semi-public locations, including community kitchen projects, art installations, or research formats in the form of collective eating events.[28]

In parallel to these thematic sessions, students followed food products from production spaces all the way through the food cycle to their own local supermarkets. Students used journal and newspaper articles, satellite imagery, industry websites, social media posts, and interviews to trace their chosen product around the globe. The items included eggs, honey, tea, bread, chicken, bananas, soy, fruit-gums, milk, and beer. Research was translated into five different mappings, illustrating: (1) the properties of the food items; (2) the item's global supply chains; (3) a network analysis of its key actors; (4) architectural drawings of one of the product stations; and (5) their locations within the city.[29] These mappings consisted of digital representations and CAD drawings of supply chains, technical drawings, network diagrams, infographics, floor plans, location plans, perspective drawings, and explanatory texts.

Going to Places and Staying at Home 35

Each mapping produced a new view on the relational nature of sites. For example, the first mapping on food processing and manufacturing showed how each item or product was in itself already a spatial composite, often made with different ingredients from different sites, or processed using specialised labour and machinery coming from different areas. The second map led students to follow the journey of products throughout the world, from production, processing, and shipping to their final distribution and sale in Cottbus, Germany (the site of our university). Figure 2.1 documents the growth of sugar beets in two regions, one in France, one in Germany. It follows the collection of the plants for processing beet sugar in southern Germany to the delivery of the sugar to another factory near the Belgian border to be turned into candy. The candy is then moved to a logistics centre, from which it is then distributed throughout Europe.[30] With this map, students learned that sites taking part in supply chains are not just spaces of production, manufacturing, or retail but also spaces of circulation.

The mapping of human and non-human actors involved in the production and sale of the products gave valuable insight into the laws, markets, regulatory frameworks, and other social constructs that govern and produce sites such as the fields, factories, and logistics centres above. The fourth and fifth mappings produced a more detailed examination of architectural structures and their locations within a given region. In some cases, these drawings helped students examine the architectures of seemingly *forgotten/overlooked key sites* in supply chains and how flows of food in the city shape urban environments. For instance, Figure 2.2 shows a critical analysis of the architectures of Darjeeling tea production, which also highlighted colonial legacies and embedded spatialities of inequality. The students mapped the various building sites in the hilly areas of Darjeeling, noting that while plantation owners enjoy renovated estates, workers must settle for simple barracks.[31]

Starting with the simple task of making food and then choosing a familiar product from their own homes, students quickly formed a conceptual, embodied connection with their research topic that moved beyond the computer screen. Conceiving and structuring the entire seminar as a journey along the different supply chain stations gave the seminar a linking narrative and transported participants to diverse spaces. Through their mappings, students strengthened their understanding of the city from a mere set of physical sites to a networked space of visible and invisible systems.[32] By examining food systems and the food supply chain, we can see how global processes are effectively embedded in particular sites and how these sites (although

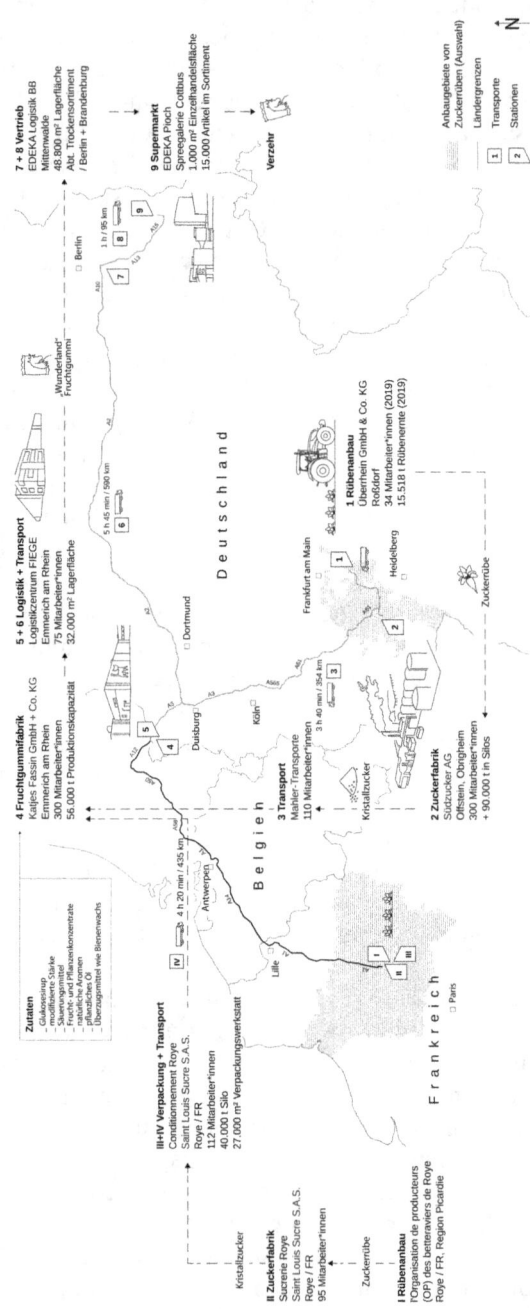

Figure 2.1 'Sugar wonderland – from the farmland to the supermarket shelf' (Daniel Cardué, Theres Marthaler, Natalie Schubert, and Lukas Teschner, 2021).

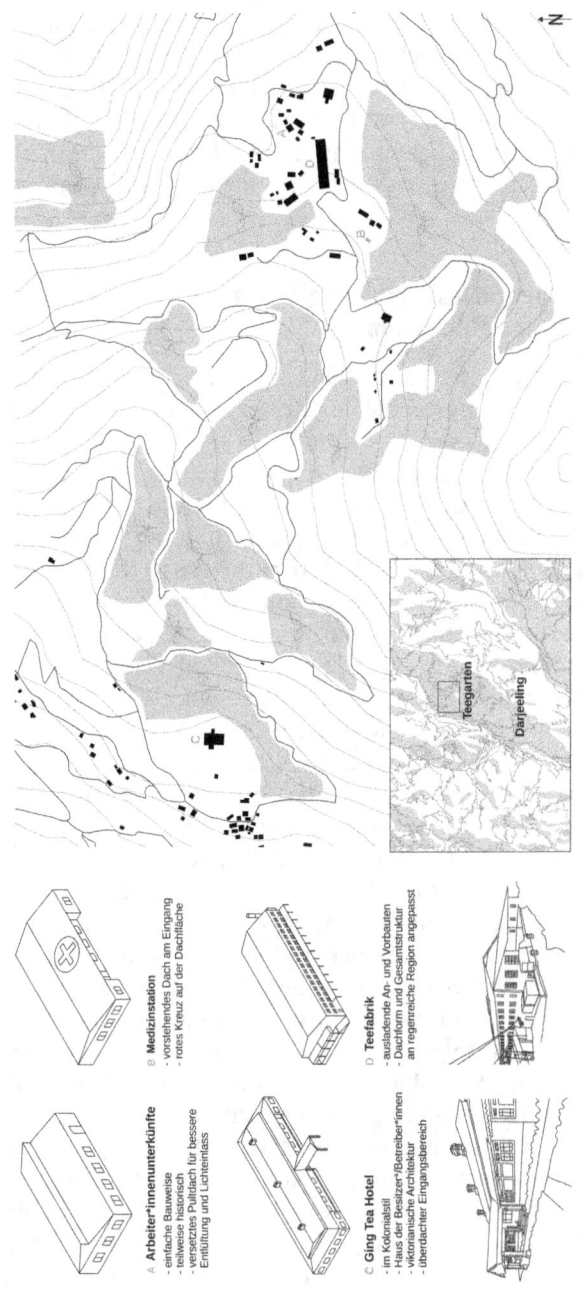

Figure 2.2 'The architectures of tea plantations in Darjeeling, India' (Julia Fritsche, Laurin Roman Henklein, Julia Theite Piro, and Leonard Zappe, 2021).

seemingly unimportant if seen isolated) are essential for the operation of translocal networks. As much as food systems produce spatialities, different sites give shape and structure to operations within food circuits. This approach helped participants reflect on the intertwined processes occurring at different scales along each supply chain station and helped link the practice of planning with socially and politically relevant issues such as ecology, cultural identity, and configurations of power relations.

Desktop Documentaries: Exposing Ways of Seeing in Online Education

That the technologies we use to view and record the world influence the way we see is a well-established argument in many disciplines and is one argued most fervently within the field of visual culture.[33] A casual glance differs from an hour spent sketching. Both approaches will produce a distinct understanding compared to that which results from the use of a camera—and even that will differ from the use of a camera phone. Seeing technologies, from the eye to the pen to the satellite, selectively mediate the information our brains receive by directing focus, filtering information, and dictating the length of the gaze. Technological innovations engender cultures of visuality. Moreover, how we see is also shaped by context: Where are we looking? In the studio or onsite? Why are we looking? For work? For pleasure? How long did we look for? For whom are we looking?

In urban planning and other spatial disciplines, matters of sight, interpretation, cognition, and their impact on design have long been of both theoretical and practical concern; it is thus unsurprising that they also fuel pedagogical debates in design education, including how students are meant to interact with the sites they are studying.[34] Schools quarrel over whether students should hand draw or use CAD software;[35] whether students should first see the site in question or rather first read secondary literature and gather pertinent historical and contextual information; to what extent, and when, students should interview and/or collaborate with users.[36] Each way of seeing yields a different understanding of the specific site.

The use of digital technologies in higher education, and above all the internet, has accelerated in the last decade as the first generation of digital natives entered university. The proliferation of different tools and technologies has been profoundly transforming the way our students see—and learn. In terms of research, students increasingly only read information that they find online, preferring downloadable articles and blog entries to anything found in a library. Some of us spend a lot of our time as educators trying to steer students away from online-only research and to teach them about credible, peer-reviewed sources; or we choose to embrace it, recognising that often, the most up-to-date information is online and comes from a variety of sources, and not just the academy. For those of us trained with pencils and sketchbooks, site visits with students can seem baffling, as very few draw or take notes unless it is explicitly required by the assignment. Rather, many students now snap a quick progression of pictures, often with their phones. They orient themselves with easily available maps and satellite images, noting already provided Points of Interest (POIs) as site context. Some students are reluctant to produce onsite documentation themselves, arguing that there are better shots of the site available on Google Images.

This over-reliance on online resources was cemented by the COVID-19 lockdowns. Students could no longer access libraries, could not visit sites, and could not meet with local actors. Rather, their data set was circumscribed to what they could find online. Students had sites to visit, but they could only look around via the internet and the information they could gather was thoroughly mediated by the computer. For this reason, for the master's studio 'From the Region', rather than assigning the final paper and presentation usually required for the course, students were encouraged to critically reflect on this limitation, on how the dependency on the computer framed both their research and project development, by executing their project as a desktop documentary.

Desktop documentaries are a type of video essay developed by the filmmaker Kevin B. Lee.[37] In them, the filmmaker uses the screen capture function to record action on their desktop as they move and manipulate different windows, programs, and content. The filmmaker builds and illustrates a narrative by pulling up content such as pictures, text, webpages, and video. For instance, one can record and exhibit dialogue in chat programs, summon others by calling them on Skype or Zoom, or write and draw in text editors and picture programs to create emphasis with keywords, diagrams, and take-away points. This form of documentary dramatises the consumption and production of information via the internet. As Lee states, it allows the author to 'seize the means of audio-visual production and circulation' and exposes how we 'learn how to express ourselves and think through-audio visual material'.[38] The result is a re-staging—and even a falsification—of the research process. Even though the film is pre-scripted and edited, we, as viewers, experience the filmmaker's journey to uncover information as though it is happening in real-time.

Video essays, of which the desktop documentary is just one type, have become an increasingly more common form of academic expression in film and media studies, visual culture, art history, and other fields concerned with the ways and means of seeing. They are increasingly taught in higher education institutes, and in 2014, *The Journal of Cinema and Media Studies* launched *[in]Transition,* the first peer-reviewed journal of academic video essays.[39] Video essays are not often, if at all, seen in urban planning. We, the instructors, assigned the desktop documentary in hopes that it would compel—or even force—the students to critically reflect on the epistemology of their research, design, and presentation practices. The assignment asked the students to analyse various aspects of the food system in the Oder-Spree, a region to the southeast of Berlin, and to create a proposal to help strengthen the development and distribution of regional products. Yet their site of research, analysis, and presentation was the computer screen itself.

In terms of pragmatics, our students had no previous experience with filmmaking or editing. A colleague at our university's Multimedia Centre gave the students a brief introduction to storytelling and shooting techniques and received no technical introduction. The teachers communicated repeatedly that expectations with regard to technical skill and filmmaking remained low; rather, students should focus on content, structure, and analysis. Most material was filmed using the screen capture function on their computer, but when students chose to film extra material they used the cameras on their mobile phones. Sound and video editing was done with QuickTime, iMovie, Adobe Premiere Pro, Audacity, and Magix Video Deluxe. The students worked in groups but remained isolated from one another, communicating solely online. The course followed a typical studio format, with students presenting their progress weekly and receiving feedback from instructors via online consultations.

Although the final outcomes differed greatly in terms of both style and content, observable similarities highlight how this experimental format impacted the learning process. First, the question of 'audience' shifted immediately. Without any intervention on behalf of the instructor, the students were quick to reimagine the audience of their semester project as the general public, as opposed to the academic community, or even more accurately, their teachers and classmates. Content and language were simplified; students laboured to make their videos entertaining as well as informative. As teachers, we followed their lead, ultimately finding that such an approach helped students to evaluate and prioritise information. Even at the postgraduate level, many students (in all disciplines really) still struggle with the transition from 'report writing', in which they report in their assignments every single detail uncovered during research as well as every single step used to develop their own ideas, to a more sophisticated form of academic writing, where information is selected, synthesised, and built to create a mature argument. Re-imagination of the audience from 'teacher' to 'potential YouTube viewer' helped our students learn how to filter information to create linearity, cohesion, and persuasion.

Limitations also became immediately apparent. Even more so due to the fact that the students were working in a relatively undocumented rural area, students quickly realised that they did not have access to all information necessary for their research. For many, this led to a change in topic—a focus on what they could discuss, not unlike what often happens in more advanced academic research. However, in the online format, this severe limitation also emboldened students to seek out information through interview partners. When something could not be found online, students brainstormed creatively how they could find that information out, calling experts, municipal workers, local businesses, community groups. One group reached a friend of a friend's grandmother and asked her to test out the duration of various bus routes. More than needed an understanding of the spatiality of their projects, the students lacked the ability to observe social life in those sites.

The assignment also provoked the students to reflect more deeply on evidence, and what it means to synthesise and analyse data in the creation of a narrative or argument. For the video essay, evidence and representative material often could be easily 'lifted' directly from an online source.[40] For example, documentary videos could be streamed; pictures and maps shown; statistics from government databases pulled up: clips from Zoom interviews replayed, and so on. However, when material was needed for a synthetic or analytic statement, it proved more challenging as there was no direct image that would illustrate what the students wished to express. Without a perfect visual, students often were compelled to falsify the source of evidence in order to show synthesis or analysis: for example, by creating their own 'websites' or 'planning documents' that included necessary maps or details, or even filming interviews with fake characters they played, in order to assume conclusive positions (Figures 2.3 and 2.4). We decided to allow these counterfeit representations, yet students were naturally conflicted about this act of misrepresentation. Their confusion and hesitation generated fruitful discussion on parallels in academic writing, and how one creates a voice of authority in analysis of other sources.

Figure 2.3 Desktop documentary with fictitious website on regional shops (Chloe Angot, Charlene Caspar, Patrick Kühlwein, Natalie Schuberg, and Lukas Teschner, 2021).

Ultimately, the desktop documentary proved an enormously helpful tool for helping our students not only reflect on limitations of that particular semester, but also for helping them understand ways of seeing, and practices of learning. They were able to critically examine the limits, pitfalls and online research and expression, and to

Figure 2.4 Desktop documentary with self-created website and fictitious interview (Julia Hübner, Belinda Kergel, Paul Lambrecht, and Gianna Mund, 2021).

brainstorm creative solutions. Most unexpectedly, the assignment greatly enhanced their understanding of the nebulous expectations and practices of scientific writing. Questions of tone, voice, audience, argumentation structure, evidence, sources, and so on were re-examined in a comparative format that helped shed light on the expectations and standard practices of academic writing.

Conclusion

Online teaching poses challenges quite distinct from traditional classroom instruction or studio work. Particularly when students are widely dispersed geographically, educators must rethink the nature of site focus in their course design. Yet, as educators try to find links and common points of departure among students joined digitally and virtually, we quickly come to a conception of site, space, and city that parallels current theorisations of the urban that go beyond material constructions to consider flows, linkages, and relationality.

In this way, online teaching's intrinsic spatial purview is decidedly global, networked, and digital and it may work best when courses are designed to examine precisely such geographic realities and to encourage new ways that students can perceive sites. As argued in this chapter, the first step in such an approach is choosing a theme which helps focus the course on planning issues with a global reach, and ideally one that can link the students into a network of analysis from their own homes. Critical mappings and the ethnographic 'follow-the-thing' method are two approaches that can guide students to research sites relationally and help challenge the concept of site as spatially fixed. By examining a global phenomenon such as the food supply chain, students linked their everyday experiences within their homes with planning-related processes that extended out of the classroom and around the globe. This methodology shifted not only their understanding of the city, but also their understanding of how one researches the networked systems and complexities of urban processes, and the limitations of that research created by digital sources, tools, and methods. Above all, online education should require students to critically reflect on the epistemology of their learning experiences. Assignments such as self-reflective mappings and desktop documentaries compel students to contemplate the means by which they were gaining and producing knowledge. Student researchers are then forced to confront research gaps, partial and biased information, and untrustworthy sources, while also navigating how to contribute responsibly to any network of knowledge.

Notes

1 See Neil Brenner and Christian Schmid, "Planetary Urbanisation," in *Urban Constellations*, ed. Matthew Gandy (Berlin: Jovis-Verlag, 2011), 10–3; Neil Brenner and Christian Schmid, "Towards a New Epistemology of the Urban?," *City* 19, no. 2–3 (May 4, 2015): 151–82, https://doi.org/10.1080/13604813.2015.1014712; Nik Heynen, Maria Kaika, and Erik Swyngedouw, eds., *In the Nature of Cities: Urban Political Ecology and the Politics of Urban Metabolism*, Questioning Cities Series (London; New York: Routledge, 2006); Colin McFarlane, "Translocal Assemblages: Space, Power and Social Movements," *Geoforum* 40, no. 4 (July 2009): 561–7, https://doi.org/10.1016/j.geoforum.2009.05.003; Colin McFarlane, "The City as Assemblage: Dwelling and Urban Space," *Environment and Planning D: Society and Space* 29, no. 4 (August 1, 2011): 649–71, https://doi.org/10.1068/d4710.
2 Two other colleagues, Anke Hagemann and Christoph Muth, were also responsible for the design and execution of these courses.
3 Saskia Sassen, "Cities Are at the Center of Our Environmental Future," *S.A.P.I.EN.S. Surveys and Perspectives Integrating Environment and Society*, no. 2.3 (December 15, 2009), http://journals.openedition.org/sapiens/948.
4 Gerrit Schwalbach, *Basics Urban Analysis*, Basics Urban Analysis (Birkhäuser, 2017), https://www.degruyter.com/document/doi/10.1515/9783035612851/html.
5 Geography has included many ways to think about space, from long standing debates between absolute views (space as container) and relative views (spaces defined in relation to other spaces, processes, bodies), to more recent ways of thinking space based on relational theory. For summaries, see: Martin Jones, "Phase Space: Geography, Relational Thinking, and Beyond," *Progress in Human Geography* 33, no. 4 (August 1, 2009): 487–506, https://doi.org/10.1177/0309132508101599 and Markus Schroer, *Räume, Orte, Grenzen: Auf Dem Weg Zu Einer Soziologie Des Raums*, 1. Aufl, Suhrkamp Taschenbuch Wissenschaft 1761 (Frankfurt am Main: Suhrkamp, 2006).
6 Ash Amin, "Re-thinking the Urban Social," *City* 11, no. 1 (April 1, 2007): 100–14, https://doi.org/10.1080/13604810701200961.
7 Jane M. Jacobs, "Urban Geographies I: Still Thinking Cities Relationally," *Progress in Human Geography* 36, no. 3 (June 2012): 412–22, https://doi.org/10.1177/0309132511421715.
8 In studying space and power in social movements, Colin McFarlane offers some orientations to understand the 'translocality' of these assemblages. He argues that translocal assemblages consist of exchanges of different kinds between situated or localised social movements across places. In this context, sites are understood as performative places where events *can* happen, making them much more than just 'nodes' or 'points' in space. Colin McFarlane, "Translocal Assemblages: Space, Power and Social Movements," *Geoforum* 40, no. 4 (July 2009): 561–7, https://doi.org/10.1016/j.geoforum.2009.05.003.
9 Amin, "Re-thinking the Urban Social." See also Ignacio Farías and Thomas Bender, eds., *Urban Assemblages: How Actor-Network Theory Changes Urban Studies*, First issued in paperback, Questioning Cities

Series (London New York: Routledge, Taylor & Francis Group, 2011); Bruno Latour, *Reassembling the Social: An Introduction to Actor-Network-Theory*, Clarendon Lectures in Management Studies (Oxford ; New York: Oxford University Press, 2005); Colin McFarlane, 'The City as Assemblage: Dwelling and Urban Space', *Environment and Planning D: Society and Space* 29, no. 4 (1 August 2011): 649–71, https://doi.org/10.1068/d4710.; Jonathan Murdoch, *Post-Structuralist Geography: A Guide to Relational Space* (London ; Thousand Oaks, Calif: SAGE, 2006).

10 Saskia Sassen, "Locating Cities on Global Circuits," *Environment and Urbanization* 14, no. 1 (April 1, 2002): 13–30, https://doi.org/10.1177/095624780201400102.

11 Amin, 'Re-thinking the Urban Social'; McFarlane, 'Translocal Assemblages'.

12 Thomas Blaschke et al., "Place versus Space: From Points, Lines and Polygons in GIS to Place-Based Representations Reflecting Language and Culture," *ISPRS International Journal of Geo-Information* 7, no. 11 (November 19, 2018): 452, https://doi.org/10.3390/ijgi7110452.

13 Mariele O'Reilly, "Constructing a Sense of Place through New Media: A Case Study of Humans of New York" (Media, Communication and Development, London, London School of Economics and Political Science, 2015), https://www.lse.ac.uk/media-and-communications/assets/documents/research/msc-dissertations/2015/Mariele-OReilly.pdf.

14 Nina Baur et al., "Theory and Methods in Spatial Analysis. Towards Integrating Qualitative, Quantitative and Cartographic Approaches in the Social Sciences and Humanities," *Historical Social Research/Historische Sozialforschung* 39, no. 2 (April 1, 2014): 15, https://doi.org/10.12759/hsr.39.2014.2.7-50.

15 Maria Kaika, *City of Flows: Modernity, Nature, and the City* (New York: Routledge, 2005).

16 Maria S. Giudici, *Architecture for Unhappy Families. Five Attempts to Rethink Dwelling through Care*, Lecture, Symposium Care-Work. Space, Bodies and the Politics of Care (Rice University, 2021), https://www.ricedesignalliance.org/video/care-work-space-bodies-and-politics-care-panel-1.

17 Dani Burrows, "Unpacking Food," in *Politics of Food*, ed. Aaron Cezar and Dani Burrows (Delfina Foundation, Sternberg Press, 2019), 12,13.

18 Steel, Carolyn Steel, *Hungry City: How Food Shapes Our Lives*, Reprint (London: Vintage, 2013).

19 Steel, ix.

20 Claus Bech-Danielsen, "The Kitchen: An Architectural Mirror of Everyday Life and Societal Development," *Journal of Civil Engineering and Architecture* 6, no. 4 (April 2012): 457–69.

21 The aesthetics, layout, and structure of the maps were based on the mapping methodology of the research seminar "Architectures of Circulation" led by Elke Beyer and Lucas Elster (TU Berlin). The rationale behind the mapping practice stemmed from the research project "Transnational Production Spaces", in which Anke Hagemann, one of the lecturers of "Feeding the City", was involved.

22 Ian Cook, "Follow the Things," accessed May 30, 2021, http://www.followthethings.com/faq.shtml. "Follow the things", a phrase coined initially in 1988 by Arjun Appadurai and expanded upon by George

Marcus in 1995, has been widely operationalised by Cook et al. Their works on food and other commodities encourage researchers and students to undertake multi-site ethnographic research related to global trade and consumption ethics. Ian Cook, "Follow the Thing: Papaya," *Antipode* 36, no. 4 (2004): 642–64, https://doi.org/10.1111/j.1467-8330.2004.00441.x; Ian Cook et al, "From 'follow the Thing: Papaya' to Followthethings.Com," April 26, 2017, https://ore.exeter.ac.uk/repository/handle/10871/26688.

23 Ian Cook, "Follow the Things," accessed May 30, 2021, http://www.followthethings.com/faq.shtml.

24 Ian Cook, "Follow the Thing: Papaya," followthethings.com, 2011, http://www.followthethings.com/followthethingpapaya.shtml Accessed May 30, 2021; Keith DellaGrotta and Meredith Weaver, "Broccoli & Desire," followthethings.com, 2011, http://www.followthethings.com/broccolianddesire.shtml. Accessed May 30, 2021; Robert Conor Burke, "Tangled Routes," followthethings.com, 2011, http://www.followthethings.com/tangledroutes.shtml. Accessed May 30, 2021.

25 Carolyn Steel, *Hungry City: How Food Shapes Our Lives* (London: Vintage, 2013).

26 In tracing the fruit, the students discovered the work of Isabella Giunta, "Food Sovereignty in Ecuador: Peasant Struggles and the Challenge of Institutionalization," *The Journal of Peasant Studies* 41, no. 6 (November 2, 2014): 1201–24, https://doi.org/10.1080/03066150.2014.938057.

27 Anke Hagemann and Natacha Quintero González, "Lebensmittelkreisläufe und die Produktion städtischer Räume," in *Feeding the city: Lebensmittelkreisläufe und die Produktion städtischer Räume*, ed. Anke Hagemann and Natacha Quintero González (Cottbus, Germany: BTU Cottbus-Senftenberg, 2021), 4, https://doi.org/10.26127/BTUOPEN-5505.

28 See Inga Reimers, "Die Stadt als Tafel: Öffentliches Essen und Kochen als Setting," *dérive*, April 2017, 67 edition, and her other works on Ess-Settings on the scholar's website. http://taktsinn.org/ess-settings/.

29 Alhadid Ajjan et al., *Feeding the city: food cycles and the production of urban space (Feeding the city: Lebensmittelkreisläufe und die Produktion städtischer Räume)*, ed. Anke Hagemann and Natacha Quintero González (BTU Cottbus – Senftenberg, 2021), https://doi.org/10.26127/BTUOPEN-5505.

30 Daniel Cardué et al., "Zucker," in *Feeding the city: food cycles and the production of urban space*, ed. Anke Hagemann and Natacha Quintero González (Cottbus, Germany: BTU Cottbus – Senftenberg, 2021), 34–40, https://doi.org/10.26127/BTUOPEN-5505.

31 Julia Fritsche et al., "Tee," in *Feeding the city: food cycles and the production of urban space*, ed. Anke Hagemann and Natacha Quintero González (BTU Cottbus – Senftenberg, 2021), 62–8, https://doi.org/10.26127/BTUOPEN-5505.

32 Maria Kaika and Erik Swyngedouw, "Radical Urban Political-Ecological Imaginaries," *Derivé/Eurozine*, May 14, 2014, https://www.eurozine.com/radical-urban-political-ecological-imaginaries/; Nik Heynen,

Maria Kaika, and Erik Swyngedouw, *In the Nature of Cities: Urban Political Ecology and the Politics of Urban Metabolism* (London: Routledge, 2006), https://doi.org/10.4324/9780203027523.

33 Most famously, John Berger explored these issues in John Berger, *Ways of Seeing* (Penguin UK, 2008). For a further consideration see, e.g.: Marita Sturken and Lisa Cartwright, *Practices of Looking: An Introduction to Visual Culture* (Oxford University Press, 2018).

34 See for instance: Mark Alan Hewitt, *Draw in Order to See: A Cognitive History of Architectural Design* (ORO Editions, 2020); Undine Giseke et al., eds., *Urban Design Methods* (De Gruyter, 2021), https://doi.org/10.1515/9783868599558.

35 Timothy Onosahwo Iyendo, "Computer Aided Design (CAD) Technology versus Students' Learning in Architectural Design Pedagogy – A Controversial Topic Review", *Computer Aided Design* 05 (2015): 7.

36 See for instance: Jamal Al-Qawasmi, *Changing Trends in Architectural Design Education* (csaar, 2006).

37 Lee's first desktop documentary, *Transformers: The Premake*, was filmed in 2014 and can be found on the artist's Vimeo page. https://vimeo.com/kevinblee

38 Kevin B. Lee, *Desktop Documentaries Tutorial with Kevin B. Lee*, 2021, accessed June 7, 2021, https://vimeo.com/500495238.

39 The journal is a collaboration between the *Journal for Cinema and Media Studies* (run by the Society for Cinema and Media Studies) and the digital network of media scholars, MediaCommons. *[in]Transition*. http://mediacommons.org/intransition/

40 In terms of existing material, the issue of copyrights proved to be a major challenge. Whether it was pictures and videos taken from the internet or their own interview clips, the students consistently had questions about how to lawfully use the material. We did not know answers, found contradictory information online, and heard different answers from our legal department and our European Data adherence office. Neither of which had the capacity to answer every possible scenario that the project posed. The project underlined the widespread problem that academics do not receive proper up-to-date training on copyright issues.

Bibliography

Amin, Ash. "Re-thinking the Urban Social." *City* 11, no. 1 (April 1, 2007): 100–14. https://doi.org/10.1080/13604810701200961.

Baur, Nina, Linda Hering, Anna Raschke, and Cornelia Thierbach. "Theory and Methods in Spatial Analysis. Towards Integrating Qualitative, Quantitative and Cartographic Approaches in the Social Sciences and Humanities." *Historical Social Research/Historische Sozialforschung* 39, no. 2 (April 1, 2014): 7–50. https://doi.org/10.12759/hsr.39.2014.2.7-50.

Bech-Danielsen, Claus. "The Kitchen: An Architectural Mirror of Everyday Life and Societal Development." *Journal of Civil Engineering and Architecture* 6, no. 4 (April 2012): 457–69.

Berger, John. *Ways of Seeing*. London: Penguin UK, 2008.
Blaschke, Thomas, Helena Merschdorf, Pablo Cabrera-Barona, Song Gao, Emmanuel Papadakis, and Anna Kovacs-Györi. "Place versus Space: From Points, Lines and Polygons in GIS to Place-Based Representations Reflecting Language and Culture." *ISPRS International Journal of Geo-Information* 7, no. 11 (November 19, 2018): 452. https://doi.org/10.3390/ijgi7110452.
Brenner, Neil, and Christian Schmid. "Planetary Urbanisation." In *Urban Constellations*, edited by Matthew Gandy, 10–3. Berlin: Jovis-Verl, 2011.
———. "Towards a New Epistemology of the Urban?" *City* 19, no. 2–3 (May 4, 2015): 151–82. https://doi.org/10.1080/13604813.2015.1014712.
Burke, Robert Conor. "Tangled Routes." followthethings.com, 2011. http://www.followthethings.com/tangledroutes.shtml.
Burrows, Dani. "Unpacking Food." In *Politics of Food*, edited by Aaron Cezar and Dani Burrows, 12–5. Delfina Foundation, Sternberg Press, 2019.
Burrows, Dani, and Aaron Cezar, eds. *Politics of Food*. London: Delfina Foundation, Berlin: Sternberg Press, 2019.
Cardué, Daniel, Theres Marthaler, Natalie Schubert, and Lukas Teschner. "Zucker." In *Feeding the City: Food Cycles and the Production of Urban Space*, edited by Anke Hagemann and Natacha Quintero González, 34–40. Cottbus, Germany: BTU Cottbus – Senftenberg, 2021. https://doi.org/10.26127/BTUOPEN-5505.
Cook, Ian. "Follow the Thing: Papaya." *Antipode* 36, no. 4 (2004): 642–64. https://doi.org/10.1111/j.1467-8330.2004.00441.x.
———. "Follow the Thing: Papaya." followthethings.com, 2011. http://www.followthethings.com/followthethingpapaya.shtml.
———. "Follow the Things." followthethings.com, 2018. http://www.followthethings.com/faq.shtml.
Cook, Ian. et al, "From 'Follow the Thing: Papaya' to Followthethings.Com." *Journal of Consumer Ethics* 1, no. 1 (April 26, 2017): 1–29.
DellaGrotta, Keith, and Meredith Weaver. "Broccoli & Desire." followthethings.com, 2011. http://www.followthethings.com/broccolianddesire.shtml.
Fischer, Edward F., and Peter Benson. *Broccoli and Desire: Global Connections and Maya Struggles in Postwar Guatemala*. Stanford: Stanford University Press, 2006.
Fritsche, Julia, Laurin R. Henklein, Julia T. Piro, and Leonard Zappe. "Tee." In *Feeding the City: Food Cycles and the Production of Urban Space*, edited by Anke Hagemann and Natacha Quintero González, 62–8. BTU Cottbus – Senftenberg, 2021. https://doi.org/10.26127/BTUOPEN-5505.
Giseke, Undine, Martina Löw, Angela Million, Philipp Misselwitz, and Jörg Stollmann, eds. *Urban Design Methods*. De Gruyter, 2021. https://doi.org/10.1515/9783868599558.
Giudici, Maria S. Architecture for Unhappy Families. Five Attempts to Rethink Dwelling through Care. *Lecture, Symposium Care-Work. Space, Bodies and the Politics of Care*. Rice University, 2021. https://www.ricedesignalliance.org/video/care-work-space-bodies-and-politics-care-panel-1.

Giunta, Isabella. "Food Sovereignty in Ecuador: Peasant Struggles and the Challenge of Institutionalization." *The Journal of Peasant Studies* 41, no. 6 (November 2, 2014): 1201–24. https://doi.org/10.1080/03066150.2014.938057.

Hagemann, Anke, and Natacha Quintero González. "Lebensmittelkreisläufe und die Produktion städtischer Räume." In *Feeding the city: Lebensmittelkreisläufe und die Produktion städtischer Räume*, edited by Anke Hagemann and Natacha Quintero González, 4. Cottbus, Germany: BTU Cottbus-Senftenberg, 2021. https://doi.org/10.26127/BTUOPEN-5505.

Hewitt, Mark Alan. *Draw in Order to See: A Cognitive History of Architectural Design*. Novato, California: ORO Editions, 2020.

Heynen, Nik, Maria Kaika, and Erik Swyngedouw, eds. *In the Nature of Cities: Urban Political Ecology and the Politics of Urban Metabolism*. Questioning Cities Series. London ; New York: Routledge, 2006.

"[In]Transition | A MediaCommons Project." Accessed February 28, 2022. http://mediacommons.org/intransition/.

Jacobs, Jane M. "Urban Geographies I: Still Thinking Cities Relationally." *Progress in Human Geography* 36, no. 3 (June 2012): 412–22. https://doi.org/10.1177/0309132511421715.

Jones, Martin. "Phase Space: Geography, Relational Thinking, and Beyond." *Progress in Human Geography* 33, no. 4 (August 1, 2009): 487–506. https://doi.org/10.1177/0309132508101599.

Kaika, Maria. *City of Flows: Modernity, Nature, and the City*. New York: Routledge, 2005.

Kaika, Maria, and Erik Swyngedouw. "Radical Urban Political-Ecological Imaginaries." *Derivé/Eurozine*, May 14, 2014. https://www.eurozine.com/radical-urban-political-ecological-imaginaries/.

Lee, Kevin B. Desktop Documentaries Tutorial with Kevin B. Lee, 2021. https://vimeo.com/500495238.

McFarlane, Colin. "The City as Assemblage: Dwelling and Urban Space." *Environment and Planning D: Society and Space* 29, no. 4 (August 1, 2011): 649–71. https://doi.org/10.1068/d4710.

———. "Translocal Assemblages: Space, Power and Social Movements." *Geoforum* 40, no. 4 (July 2009): 561–7. https://doi.org/10.1016/j.geoforum.2009.05.003.

O'Reilly, Mariele. "Constructing a Sense of Place through New Media: A Case Study of Humans of New York." Media, Communication and Development, London School of Economics and Political Science, 2015. https://www.lse.ac.uk/media-and-communications/assets/documents/research/msc-dissertations/2015/Mariele-OReilly.pdf.

Reimers, Inga. "Die Stadt als Tafel: Öffentliches Essen und Kochen als Setting." *dérive*, April 2017, 67 edition.

Sassen, Saskia. "Cities Are at the Center of Our Environmental Future." *S.A.P.I.EN.S. Surveys and Perspectives Integrating Environment and Society*, no. 2.3 (December 15, 2009). http://journals.openedition.org/sapiens/948.

———. "Locating Cities on Global Circuits." *Environment and Urbanization* 14, no. 1 (April 1, 2002): 13–30. https://doi.org/10.1177/095624780201400102.

Schroer, Markus. *Räume, Orte, Grenzen: Auf Dem Weg Zu Einer Soziologie Des Raums*. *1*. Aufl. Suhrkamp Taschenbuch Wissenschaft 1761. Frankfurt am Main: Suhrkamp, 2006.

Schwalbach, Gerrit. Basics Urban Analysis. Basics Urban Analysis. *Birkhäuser*, 2017. https://www.degruyter.com/document/doi/10.1515/9783035612851/html.

Steel, Carolyn. *Hungry City: How Food Shapes Our Lives*. London: Vintage, 2013.

Sturken, Marita, and Lisa Cartwright. *Practices of Looking: An Introduction to Visual Culture*. New York: Oxford University Press, 2018.

3 Sites of Alternate Origin
Design Ideation Under a New Austerity

Sean Burns and Matthew Wilson

Prelude

Design students often regard 'site' as a tangible, protected, and hallowed milieu. Within an architectural design studio, the location of a chosen site may prohibit any chance for field studies. Further, the opportunity to visit a site became a challenge during the global pandemic and lockdown, for such physical spaces were no longer directly accessible for in-person visits and analysis. As physical space might be deemed inaccessible to students, this ostensibly opens an opportunity to investigate alternate conceptions of site.

This chapter sets off with a survey of how leading scholars interpret the notion of site, territory, ground, and terrain as a physical construct. Thereafter, it contrasts absolute, neutral, and normative notions of site, ground, object, and topography with engendered, surrogate conditions by exploring how these theories relate to thinking about alternatives to such conventions. It explores different pedagogical approaches to develop projects that were executed prior to and during the pandemic. Before the pandemic, students explored an alternative construct of site in which they generated a response to an inherited architectural artefact that was situated on an accessible and physical landscape. During the pandemic, emphasis was placed on the invention of site as different inter- and multi-disciplinary media interactions to produce an evolutionary body and to explore its many implicit and explicit qualities.

The authors present site as instances of engagement with the fields of material studies and visual culture, literature and philosophy, and social and environmental justice and sociology. Here, projects speak of design ideation under a new austerity. Sites of alternate origin offer a high-level of nuanced complexity, adaptation, and rigor to expand students' views about the future of architecture. They speak to a pedagogy of site values, or about creating things worth cultural value, worth protecting, and worth caring for.

Inquiry into Site as a Physical Construct of Atmospheric Ascent

In his matrix of spatialities, David Harvey defines *absolute* 'material space' as streets, walls, territorial markers, and physical boundaries.[1] Although Harvey suggests multiple readings of space, from the lived-relative to conceptualized-relational, designers often think of site and building in *absolute* terms. A recent study by Pier Vittorio Aureli, for instance, argues for an *'absolute* architecture' in which the object or form is distinct from 'the other', or the site, 'the space of the city, its extensive organization, and its government'.[2] Patrik Schumacher has likewise declared that the 'organization and articulation of the built environment cannot proceed without the profession of architects and no other social power can determine its final shape'.[3] Yet, for Schumacher, architecture must remain 'apolitical' to uphold the status quo of superstar architecture remaining 'progressive' and 'relevant'. Indeed, interest in the architectural object as icon, spectacle, and paradigm in popular culture has its ebbs and flows.[4] Such discourse is reminiscent of late modernist attitudes from the 1960s that pitted countermodernist works concerned with region, site, and atmospheres against corporate international style architecture and its 'object fixation'.[5] This object line of thinking is typically attributed to Le Corbusier's declaration of 'Libération du sol'. The premise formed the basis of his Maison Citrohan and, later, Unité d'habitation, which was the epitome of an architecture 'emancipated from the ground'.[6]

In so far as the ground is concerned, it might be said that it is not first the architect but the imperious cartographer who inscribes the human imprint upon the natural world. Through lines, cartographers reduce the landscape to a series of discrete objects. A critique of these object-oriented positions is that they are too limited in their application as an *absolute* dichotomy of architectural object vs 'the other'. Michael Hensel argues that lines should not be limited by this notion of the absolute, however. He poses the question: 'Does the delineation of items contradict the possibility of continuity and connectivity? And can their correlation begin to indicate a different attitude towards ground?'.[7] This paper seeks to pose the same question as it relates to the conceptual intersection of the words site, ground, foundation, and territory. Consider, for instance, such thinking as it relates to the works of John Rajchman, who states:

> 'Ground' is a word like 'foundation', with uses in both philosophy and architecture suggesting some deep analogy or affinity between the two. More modestly, the word may be said to have a conceptual potential that one can exploit to suggest new ways of thinking and perhaps also of building.[8]

Along these lines, the global pandemic has forced us to recognize material site as a localized empirical experience. As suggested above, it forced instructors of architectural design studios into 'remote' learning environments, where site visits became impossible and instructors were forced to rethink that, among other aspects of the design curriculum. As David Leatherbarrow astutely noted years before the pandemic, 'contemporary technology' may 'emancipate design from the practical and environmental'.[9] And during the pandemic, the contemporary technology of architectural zooming became the new norm.

The remote studio of the pandemic vaguely calls to mind the metaphysical posturing of myriad 'progressive' paperless or virtual architects of the late 1990s and 2000s. At that time, however, some of its main protagonists still put emphasis on site. As Greg Lynn once noted, the 'earth is conceived as a porous mass capable of supporting objects not only on its surface, but also burrowing and floating within its mass, then a new sense of ground has been established and a new mobility achieved'.[10] Soon enough, though, the design world moved on to more burning questions: a turn to the issues of sustainability, hyper-densification, post-industrialism, and the post-digital occurred over the subsequent decades. Here one sees the integration of landscape, architecture, planning, and ecology, as opposed to architecture alone, as a multi-scalar ordering system for the contemporary city.[11] Contemporary architects have increasingly eschewed the insular architectural object for explorations of various ways of engaging the ground. As an extension of OMA's infrastructuralist principles from the 1990s, where buildings were 'allotted to the domain of infrastructure', Andreas and Ilka Ruby critique the 'conventional hierarchies' of the architectural object in order to dismantle the 'conventional hierarchies of wall, ceiling, and floor'.[12]

Yet, to recall the Rajchman quote above, emphasis on both architecture and site has remained on material culture, as opposed to, say, intellectual culture. One could consider a site, or the ground and architecture, as something more than 'material space'; it should also embrace contextual associations and representational properties. As Edouard Glissant notes, the 'poetics of landscape, which is the source of creative energy, is not to be directly confused with the physical nature of the country. Landscape retains the memory of time past. Its space is open or closed to its meaning'.[13] For Gevork Hartoonian, we 'no longer understand the classical language of architecture as pre-modern architects did; nor do we understand a building as an integral part of a coherent ensemble. Modernization disintegrated every kind of totality underlining the process of making artefacts as a formative theme of architecture'.[14] As Hartoonian states the 'subject of theatricality is important ... as a communicative dimension of architecture' that has 'changed since the crisis of the object induced by modernization and the introduction of new technologies into the process of architectural production'.[15]

During the pandemic, contemporary technology detached design studio culture from site. Similar to Marc Augé's comments on 'non-places' and the decentred self, we were ensnared in lockdown, living rather oddly in an 'intellectual, musical, or visual environment that is wholly independent' of sites of creation.[16] The implications here on the future of the design profession are worth pondering, as architecture corroborates with, and is experienced through what Dubord, Baudrillard, or Marcuse might call the one-dimensional 'image industry' of fleeting spectacles on social media, television, enterprise video communications, the home cinema, or the webshop window.[17] It is worth noting that William Mitchell once speculated about the liberating prospects of contemporary technology to create an e-topia.[18] Perhaps that vision is worth reassessment.

The pandemic has realized, it seems, the negative dialectic, an e-dystopian condition—where home quarantine amounts to the alienating business as usual.[19] The past several months of our global pandemic point to a *new normal*: a *new austerity* that demanded a full retreat from mass gatherings in which developers can speculate on, for instance, the Olympic consumption of new spectacles for the resuscitation of declining urban areas across the Western hemisphere. This 'new austerity' amounted not only to 'the quarantine' period; it is dispatching broader long-term economic, industrial, and social repercussions. The authors cannot pretend to heroically address this wider global crisis. Instead this chapter explores its adverse effects within the architectural academy and beyond, with an interest in opportunities for conceptual exploration. We write this chapter with the knowledge in mind that various plagues, war-time catastrophes, great recessions, environmental calamities, and other austerity-inducing periods have given architects various reasons to take pause and to reflect. Such periods of architectural theorizing or 'just traditional' scholarship, as opposed to the orthodox tradition of 'progressive' business as usual, tend to open possibilities for change.[20]

This work expands upon Leatherbarrow's messages of how 'contemporary technology' may emancipate designers from the tangible, 'practical and environmental' conditions of site.[21] It contends that notions of site should include such topics as literature, philosophy, history, film, or fine art. In this regard, one may re-territorialize the Deluzian notions of ground and foundation to consider sites of alternate origin relative to what Harvey, aforementioned, calls 'conceptualized spaces'.[22] Yet, questions remain as to whether the concept of site might only exist in terms of its inclusion of ground and topography. Here, Leatherbarrow argues that the nexus of architecture and landscape is topography. He offers six decisive characteristics of this relationship:

> Its character is horizontal, that movement within it continually confronts contrary conditions and mosaic heterogeneity; *that it cannot be equated with land or materials as physical substances*; that it is not form either, when that is taken to be immaterial volume or profile; that its manner of presenting itself is paradoxical: manifestly latent, or given, not shown; and that its temporality allows it to serve as both record of and invitation to human praxis, a chronicle and condition of human freedom.[23]

Effectively, site cannot be reduced solely to physical territorial boundaries: a plot of land on which we build, a demarcated boundary on the earth's surface, a limitation on atmospheric ascent, or a constraint on its penetrable depth. Instead, the authors argue that new immaterial and abstract physical ways of conceptualizing site could augment the architectural design process—by seeking to recover its essence. It urges designers to reposition and redefine their notions of site as a set of contextual parameters, whereby site is activated as a developing entity, simultaneously capable of persuading and reacting to any architectural imposition placed upon, within, or beyond its formation. As such, a project's situation, among its predetermined metes and restrictive confines—or positioning among the X,Y, and Z axes—may no longer be considered synonymous with site. These ideas about site emerged prior to the pandemic. Let us now turn to how this thinking informed case studies in the architectural design studio.

Addressing Territory and the Tolerance of Boundary

Territory implies a division of land or space to allocate isolated confines among disparate participants. These divisions are predicated upon various circumstantial motivations including: economic, political, social, national, religious, and/or natural conditions. Regarding architecture, territory is, regrettably, accepted as a native constraint imposed upon a site to segregate its configuration into two-dimensional parcels and along its three-dimensional compositional stratum. Consequently, the ground is often the instrument upon which these metes and boundary conditions are imposed and enforced. Therefore, to question the specificities of a territory requires one to examine the motives behind such imposed separations, as well as to interrogate the boundary conditions that define its limits.

Vittorio Gregotti argues that, the 'worst enemy of modern architecture is the idea of space, considered solely in terms of economic and technical exigencies indifferent to the ideas of the site...before placing stone on stone, man placed the stone on the ground to recognize a site in the midst of an unknown universe: in order to take account of it and modify it'.[24] Within his introductory description of *Augmented Landscapes*, Mark Smout and Laura Allen states that 'Man continues to mark the land, relentlessly shaping the surface from wilderness to cultivation'. [25] Here, Allen presents five design scenarios where the physical nature and properties of a site might be exploited and transformed, as a response to any proposed mediating architectural manoeuvres relative to its perceived territorial bounds. Among each of these situational studies, Allen promotes criteria for the successful integration of architecture about its accompanying site:

> The resulting architectural interventions respond to their dynamic and fluxing territories. The ephemeral character of the environment is reflected in the solidity of the artefacts that inhabit it as they take on a local specificity and lend to their surroundings a sense of nature illuminated.[26]

These assertions by Gregotti and Allen both challenge the notion that a territory is a governing and permanent article as a registrational divide between architectural design and the natural environment in which it resides. Further, Bernard Cache contends that, '...the surface of a territory is mobile and fluid as it is given to the distortions of memory'.[27] This argument implies that a territory should no longer be strictly fixed, but instead it might be seen as a set of conditional

Sites of Alternate Origin   57

peripheries or limitable bounds—unpredictable in their demarcation, duration, and influence for a precarious site.

On this line of thinking, a cohort of undergraduate architectural design studio students were presented with a project inviting each of them to investigate the misgivings of boundary conditions, the limits of situational edges, and the vulnerabilities of territorial environments as applicable measures for architectural design. The project asked students to inherit the site of the abandoned Empire Quarry in Vallonia, Indiana, which during the early twentieth century provided over 18,000 tons of limestone to aid in the construction of the Empire State Building in New York City, New York, as well as several other national monuments. Specific to the project's requirements, students were directed to design and develop a visitor centre to educate the public about the site's heritage through an architectural intervention among, beyond, and/or within the volatile, existing land formations of the abandoned quarry. Of importance here was that the assignment prompted students to reflect upon the role and meaning of 'heritage', with respect to the provided site, to advance its programme.

One important line of thinking here was that of Hamdy EL-Setouhy. This Egyptian architect conveys that the conceptual parameters of heritage are that of identity, culture, and civilization, where identity is an intangible status and culture is a persistent expression of a society's products. Further, he states that architectural heritage is 'a product of culture, and a witness to the civilization that was at the time of its creation', instead of an instigating agent of an inherent site.[28] Thus, heritage should not be restricted solely to conservation processes in an effort to preserve the historical cultural importance of a site's past, but should also strive to present insights for its future.

After researching and presenting their observations about the site, students engaged in discussion and debate towards collectively agreeing that the violent disruptions emanating from the aggressive excavations of the site's strata exposed the native and regional geological substance of its historical character. Unfortunately, the mining of massive portions of limestone-rich ground at the site led to a disturbance of its preceding heritage. In its current condition, the fabric of the earth was no longer desirable or seamless with its surroundings. Instead, the quarried land was compromised by several excavated scars among its terrain, dictating a divorce of the site from its proximate environment. Thus, the choice to quarry the earth transfigured the ground's composition as a neglected and abandoned site for the project, simultaneously activating a series of territorial boundary situations about the three-dimensional stratum of the earth and along its two-dimensional perimeter. Ultimately, the territorial divide for this site was born out of the dissection among its natural and disturbed substance and surface conditions.

As students began their designs, they were encouraged to challenge these historically imposed territorial boundaries among the earth's surface to create a unique narrative for how their proposed visitor centre might advance the heritage of the site and blur the observed strict demarcations of the ground's substance into a setting of gradient peripheries. To promote interruptions about these territorial divides, students were encouraged to further carve into the earth's substrate, but not infill these voids with architectural elements. Instead, they were persuaded to absorb these cavernous spaces as part of their designed visitor centre as instances to educate the public for their proposal (Figure 3.1).

For reference, students were introduced to the architectural theories of tectonics and stereotomy. In his treatise *Style in the Technical and Tectonic Arts: or Practical Aesthetics* (1860), Gottfried Semper discussed these terms, relative to architectural design. Semper defines tectonic elements as 'the frame with corresponding filling, the lattice as a complicated frame, the supports, and the structure as an integral support with the accompanying frame'.[29] Further, Semper pronounces the tectonic as 'the highest and most universal theme of architecture', while relegating stereotomy to methods of construction instead of a characteristic of architectural design. For Semper, stereotomic procedures are 'strictly considered, a secondary technique...its materials are not those in which the pure functional-formal theme was originally and primarily embodied'.[30] Kenneth Frampton follows Semper's assertions by emphasizing the properties of materials and expected duration of its configuration as either a permanent stereotomic manoeuvre or the additive process to erect a transient tectonic system. Robin Evans challenges these assertions that stereotomy might be reduced to a construction process. Instead, Evans suggests that stereotomy might be acknowledged as a subtractive design operation, akin to its etymological definition as the science of cutting solids. Juan José Castellón González and Pierluigi D'Acunto support Evan's claim:

> ...if the tectonic approach puts the emphasis on the constructive and technical aspects of the building and on the expression of the detail, the stereotomic approach is grounded on the generation of the voids and on the definition of the boundaries of the building. In this way, the accumulation and distribution of matter produces at the same time both space and structure.[31]

Sites of Alternate Origin 59

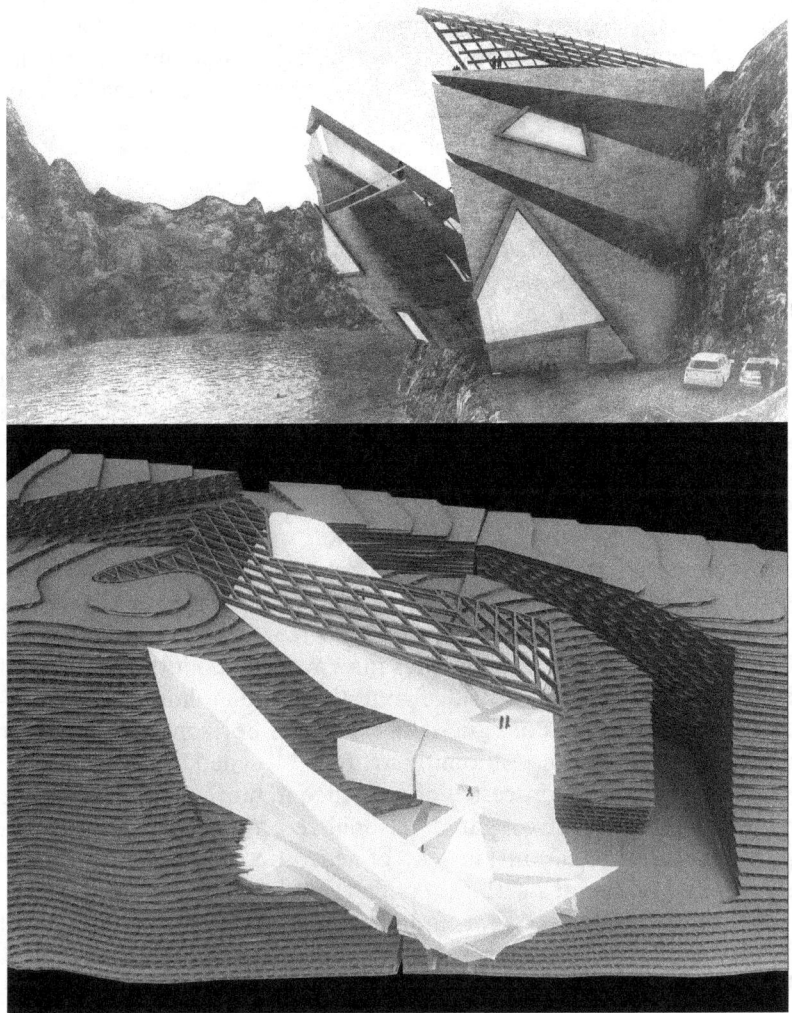

Figure 3.1 Empire Quarry by Alex Tyson.

The project challenged students to reconsider the divisive and accepted notions of territory and boundaries among a damaged and vacated site, scarred by the historical disruption of the terrain and ground's substance. The new visitor centre presented an opportunity for the students to challenge notions of generality and continuity of architecture and site.³² Instead of stitching an architectural intervention into the surrounding fabric of the earth to preserve its current identity, students deployed subtractive and additive operations based on their respective comprehension of tectonic and stereotomic theories to revise the narrative of the earth's current fabric and celebrate its heritage.

Pre-Pandemic Reconsiderations of Site

As stated above, Leatherbarrow argues that architecture and landscape share a common bond. Topography serves as the medium to forge a plastic relationship between architecture and landscape. Instead of being neglected and relegated as a remnant of architectural design, site becomes paramount to architecture's impressions upon the physical realm, where topography is advanced to the status of a situational event that reveals the various constraints and opportunities of a site or groundscape. Therefore, site is a pliant surface and/or malleable substance that indexes this dialogue between architecture and landscape. Relative to Leatherbarrow's six resolute characteristics that define the common relationship between architecture and landscape, this chapter challenges his first, and perhaps the most manifest, of these conditions: that topography is horizontal in its absolute state. Indeed, topography communicates information about the profile and face of a site's mediated surface condition. The authors argue, however, that site can be configured as a mesh of horizontal, vertical, or oblique surfaces, compositionally arranged to encourage a response to contextual forces, processes of growth, and movement. Prior to the pandemic, students investigated, rationalized, and interpreted site as a series of unique situations, instead of generating an object, independent of any associations with the context.

A project entitled 'Room and [bill]Board' charged architectural design students to reinterpret and redefine the properties of site. Here, site is emboldened by a *situational* inquiry, whereby students inherit a billboard as a non-architectural device. They were prompted to deconstruct and reimagine the material surface components and systematic tectonic frames to create a series of inhabitable volumetric spaces. Their design reorganized and adapted these elements to accommodate various programmatic events, including a photographer's studio, house, and gallery. Thus, the terrain of intervention becomes a *situation* that entertains material reconfigurations. The project encouraged students to address all horizontal, vertical, or obliquely oriented surfaces and components of the constructed artefact as the site.

Sites of Alternate Origin 61

Figure 3.2 Room and [bill]Board by Camden Hochgesang and Brian Cruz.

Prior to beginning the project, students were introduced to various architectural theories of tectonics and stereotomic processes pertaining to architectural design. They were asked to deploy and graphically communicate a series of descriptive operations as sequential, and instigative, design manoeuvres to transform the site, from an existing two-dimensional billboard into a three-dimensional multi-layered series of colliding volumetric spaces (Figure 3.2). The consequence of these manoeuvres encouraged students to develop interwoven circulatory arteries, to rearticulate the inherited tectonic assemblies to refine spatial configurations, and to offer systematic structural support instances among their respective design solutions. Upon completion of the project, students dismantled the existing billboard, as an object, and moved towards developing an architectural intervention among the situation of a non-architectural artefact.

Further, if we consider the landscape as a series of variegated profile lines across a site, the figurated object of architecture can be read as an extension of the ground plane, in contrast to an object that engages the horizon and occupies the sky. Thus, architecture—when perceived as a container, whether above or below this divisional line of the earth, might be inhabited, consumed, and unbuilt over time. Here, one might draw reference to the work of anthropologist Tim Ingold who imagines the world as a composition of entangled and engaging lines. Ingold presents this theoretical framework to better comprehend, appreciate, and study the behavioural patterns of life's processes of growth and movement. For Ingold, the concept of threads and traces are categories of lines, where threads are filaments woven together, through an additive process, to hatch a surface.[33] In contrast, traces are subtractive lines that are embedded into an existing surface, likened to indexical trace evidence, or as footprints in a snowy field, that act to weaken or destroy its integrity. Lines therefore are the means to create growth models, one of which is the container. Ingold defines this model of the container as a 'composite assembly comprised of two or more entities, where there is a clearly defined interior and exterior space delineated by the surface condition between these defined environments'.[34] In this regard (lines) traces can dissolve the object fixation (container) of modernism. Many new lines (threads) may also construct a new postmodern, pluralistic reality.

As the philosopher Jean-François Lyotard explained, postmodernity is synonymous with a confident scepticism about Enlightenment values in which the 'grand narrative' of the progress of rationality, science, industry, and technological innovation will ultimately alleviate all social troubles and personal issues.[35] Along these lines, postmodernism in the Western world is characterized by urban decline, post-industrialization, post-Fordism, leisure and consumption as ideology, climate change, 'too big to fail' capitalism, cultural flattening, and university life as preparation for corporate elitism.[36] Some scholars narrowly think of 'postmodern architecture' as a stylistic phenomenon of American classicism dating from the 1970s to the late 1990s. Yet, this treatment has come to be known as 'Postmodern classicism'.[37] This style does not encapsulate the totality of our postmodern era.[38] Along this vein, postmodern architectural theory is interdisciplinary, and new narratives have been constructed from political, ethical, linguistic, aesthetic, and phenomenological positions.[39] Thus, since announcing the 'death of modernism' with Pruitt-Igoe in 1972, Charles Jencks wrote extensively on the various schools of postmodernism, not limited to neo-vernacular, ad-hocism, and metaphysical groups.[40] They share a common bond of communicating double coding, or 'the combination of Modern techniques with something else ... in order for architecture to communicate with the public'.[41]

In one such instance of a de-coding exercise, students were charged with designing a utopian 'Po-Mo Church'. Here they sought to incorporate two remnant walls of an abandoned neo-gothic church, built in an American rust-belt 'no-where' town, into a comprehensive skate park plan. Thus only two surfaces of what Ingold might call the 'container' remained. To engage with this situational site, students introduced subtractive 'traces' that were embedded into the existing surface conditions of the ground, facade ruins, and solid/void conditions, to weaken its geometric formation as a container and dismantle its association with conservative cultural values. Students

Sites of Alternate Origin 63

Figure 3.3 Po-Mo Church by Allison Gerardot, Roberto Medina, Camden Hochgesang, and Derek Burks.

then introduced additive 'threads' independent of, but responsive to, these scarred remains to entertain a series of new programmatic events, which included skateboard shop and rampscape, a multimedia area, art gallery, studio, food hub, and sleeping pods (Figure 3.3). In this sense, students deployed 'traces' and 'threads' that embodied a radical postmodern surface tapestry of values, tactics, and tropes in the design process. They aimed to address a situational 'non-site' by 'manufacturing meaning' for a new gathering space that speaks to alternative identities, classes, and tastes, in a pluralistic fashion that undermines the rigid expectations of the container that once was.[42] Students sought to create a peripheral incubator of sociability and socio-cultural change and a means to foster diverse collectives for improving the world together.[43] Students were encouraged to act as radical postmodernists—to be 'magpie-like' in their use of references, forms, and surface tapestries—to engage the site.[44] Highly creative projects employed the formal tropes of fragmentation and imitation, the communicative tactics of counterpoint contextualism, and an expression of social values offering critique and collaboration. They developed a parasitic collage and bricolage, with the intention to create a constellation of urban micro-utopian spaces for disinvested urban populations. Along these lines Nathaniel Coleman notes that as 'no-place', 'Utopia imagines how the past can be surrendered to the future by way of renewed — reimagined — tradition'.[45]

The Paradigm of Pandemic-Engendered Sites

During the pandemic, students were prompted to explore sites of alternate origin, or design ideation under a new austerity. They drew upon the more unorthodox qualities of the notion of site, as opposed to the absolute properties of material space, to generate a design unique solution. The complications posed by the pandemic alienated them from one another and from the notion of site. It rendered futile the normative process of engaging in dialogues of site, ground, and topography. Questions arose as to when to introduce site, and whether site is a series of responsive conditions that unfold in a sequential manner to architects throughout the design process. The pandemic encouraged architects to re-examine the responsibilities of site, its accepted association as a directive agent of architectural design, and the order by which designers might accept, investigate, interpret, and respond to its conditional parameters. Rather than cling to the notion of transposing an object onto the ground, on the basis of a superficial engagement with a site's context, the pandemic offered an opportunity to explore alternatives. Here, a series of design exercises prompted students to envision, design, and fabricate their own site, thereby encouraging them to abandon their preconceived ideas about the relationship between landscape and architecture. Advancing the notion of site as a *situation* urges student architects to think of it as a series of constraints and opportunities, instead of a sacred article that is localized and defined through its metes, boundaries, and profile conditions. Herein, site might be liberated from these encoded qualities and instead be activated through alternative media (whether literature, philosophy, history, film, or fine arts). Under such guiding principles, designers interpret and deduce the associated messages of terrain, topography and, ultimately, site. Based on this premise, site is evolutionary. It continually repositions itself and emerges as a living body that exists and enters the state of 'perpetual becoming'.[46]

For a proposed site as entity, it must transcend its status to that of an active participant throughout the design process. Here student designers are prompted to reconsider the compositional strata of site as a soft, negotiable mass inspired by the philosophical teachings of Denis Diderot, who deemed all matter as 'irritable or sensible' in nature.[47] Responding to Diderot's message, designers should no longer engage the iterative design process by solely considering architecture as the agitator upon an inflicted field. Instead, they should strategically seek out methods to prolong the dialogue between site and any architectural interference, in order to best capture and define spatial

Sites of Alternate Origin 65

configurations within, among, and beyond site as a created substance. A project entitled 'Instigating Mass' expands upon Diderot's lessons, for students were asked to employ multiple design operations to physically realize a hypothetical site as a plaster cast. They were probed to study the various formational profiles and voided confines of their created site towards introducing a hierarchical system of tectonic framework assemblies. As these systems emanated from the permeable site, they served multiple functionalities. At various moments, the tectonic framework assemblies were deployed to offer structural support to the casted site; while at other instances, the linear elements aided to define volumetric spaces within or beyond the site's mass. Students were asked to adjoin their tectonic systems to the malleable site 'sympathetically,' as defined by Lars Spuybroek, by 'what things feel when they shape one another'.[48] The presentation of this theory encouraged students to continually mature and reshape their site in response to the intended deployment of tectonic assemblies throughout the duration of the design process. Thus, through the 'Instigating Mass' project, site was embodied as a designed, fabricated, and persuasive agent throughout the entirety of the design process (Figure 3.4a).

These observations and associated student projects demonstrate that sites of engagement are not limited to the absolute materiality of the urban, suburban, rural, and the like. They might include sites that are other materials. Or they might be sites of contemplation that are emotional, political, historical, philosophical, literary, and conceptual.[49] Yet, is it possible to invert this relationship, where architecture becomes the impetus for extending the literary and philosophical when it is considered a site of engagement? One such opportunity can be found in the existentialism of Jean-Paul Sartre. Sartre's one-act play entitled 'Huis Clos' is often considered the finest expression of existentialism. The play has three main protagonists. Garcin, Estelle, and Inez have all recently died, and they will spend eternity together confined in a drawing room, which contains three pieces of furniture and a large bronze 'contraption' on the mantelpiece. During the course of the play, the protagonists reveal to each other the significant faults within their lives, (i.e. the reasons they have been sent to this room for eternity). They begin to seek validation from one another for their life-choices, and they thus lose their freedom as individuals or subjects. This realization leads Garcin to claim at the end of the play, 'Hell is — other people'.[50]

Undergraduate architectural design studio students analysed this text to establish a deep appreciation of each protagonist's habits, spatial needs, and desires. They find that throughout the play, the protagonists

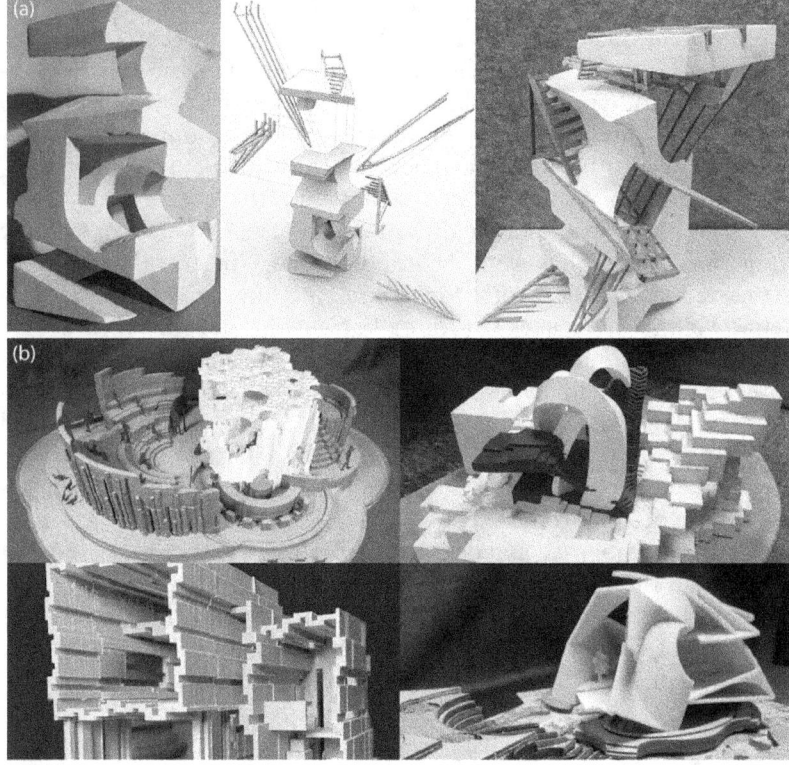

Figure 3.4 (a) top row, 'Instigating Mass' by Jake Nolan, and (b) bottom two rows, 'Huis Clos' by Jack Leibham, Carson Vaal, Mini Liard, and Keith Carrasquilla.

complain of the architecture and the objects in the room. One can imagine, however, that over time they adapt to it. Charged with outlining a scheme for a second unwritten act of 'Huis Clos', students create a collection of new 'virtual' private and public spaces for unsettling the three protagonists. Thereafter students were promoted to adapt their designs to a real but relatively inaccessible site on a body of water in a rust-belt town. They were charged with transforming their newly created living spaces (for the second act) into a floating theatre, where the protagonists may be forever watched by the townspeople (Figure 3.4b). In this way, students used architecture as the vehicle to extend the site of engagement, 'Huis Clos'. In both these projects—'Instigating Mass' and 'Huis Clos'—site is a fabricated body that students have to design and recreate, and it is relatively non-locational.

Site as Political and Social Mediascape

In another set of explorations, site may be deemed a landscape of political and social memory. As we recall the Glissant commentary above, it is the 'poetics of landscape' which 'retains the memory of time past' and that is the source of 'creative energy'.[51] Landscape is replete with memory of the racial oppression of people of colour in America. Among such artefacts are the 'door of no return' and the diaspora of Africans to the plantation fields of slavery, building the nation's Capitol and the like, and into American Civil War refugee camps, out of sundown towns, along migration pathways to the north and west, and on to the Jim Crow spaces of work, play, worship, and learn. Today, the legacy of discrimination continues to dominate American life as per the effects of redlining, racial covenants, social alienation, revised voting districts, the prison-industrial complex, gentrification schemes, the siting of toxic waste facilities and other locally unwanted land uses, and other avenues. The gradual erasure of the oppressive detritus of Jim Crow and gentrification landscapes, without reparations, are an attempt to conceal the historical truth. As Walter Hood notes, 'Erasure allows people to forget, particularly those whose lives are complicit'.[52] Recognizing sites of racial violence, and opening meaningful conversations about the past, is perhaps one route to racial justice and reparations paid forward to the descendants of the people of colour who built the United States of America.

For several decades, scholars have argued that to take a liberal stance of neutrality or to remain silent is to deny our ugly past. Academics in law, race relations, sociology, and other fields have consistently shown how the joint efforts of governmental institutions, corporations, planners, architects, and engineers have afflicted people of colour. Grass roots activists, architecture critics, and environmental justice scholars have shown how poor people and people of colour in America have been denied equal access to the basic human rights of clean water, sanitation, parks, healthcare, education, libraries, employment counselling, voting booths, public transport, and wholesome food. Instead poor people and people of colour have been disproportionately overburdened with the siting of waste incinerators, refineries, toxic waste dumps, leaded water supplies, fertilizer plants, wastewater treatment plants, and other locally unwanted land uses in their neighbourhoods.[53]

All too often, theorists, academics, and leading practitioners have remained silent, and seemingly complacent, with the prevailing monocultural, Eurocentric perspectives that avoid the connections between politics, race, and space in design education and practice. They ask: 'What role does design really play in such conversations, if anything at all?', especially when it comes to architectural education. In architectural history, for instance, that amounts to focusing on aesthetic frameworks rooted in Hegelian tropes as opposed to analysing architecture as a product of social, political, and economic relations.[54] The authors maintain, however, that all knowledge is political. 'Neutral' daily institutional practices embody 'white norms'.[55] There is inherently no such thing as a 'neutral' or 'objective' practice in legal studies, the main stream media, or even architecture. It is impossible, for instance, to turn on a television, to scroll social media feeds, or to watch a film without concluding that politics, race, and space are inherently intertwined. Those who cry for the neutrality of architecture cast it as an empirical science, an irreverent formalistic practice of art for art's sake, or just letting the invisible hand of the market do its thing.[56] But in 2020, the deaths of George Floyd, Rayshard Brooks, Ahmaud Arbery, Breonna Taylor, and the protests of the Black Lives Matter movement spurred architecture student groups to demand that their departmental administrators decentre whiteness in the design curriculum.[57]

It is not clear, however, how many academics pledged to decolonize their lectures and studio assignments. But scholars of architecture have increasingly published works that place race at the centre of design thinking and practice.[58] One example within the scholarship of teaching and learning in architecture was a graduate level, multidisciplinary architectural design studio at Ball State University in Muncie, Indiana. In the autumn of 2020, the architecture department offered a studio seeking to re-centre histories of design for Black communities. Partnering with undergraduate student-stakeholders from an 'Race and Ethnic Relations' sociology course led by Dr John Anderson Jr, the graduate architectural design students created a 'Museum of American Violence'. Graduates led online discussion sessions on such matters as the culture of power, the pathology of privilege, and how race is inherently social and shapes individual narratives, identities, social structures, institutions, and the possibilities of change.[59] They came to understand race as a social construction in which one does 'not come into this world African or European or Asian; rather this world comes into you'.[60]

The team-based collaboration, 'Museum of American Violence', took the form of a constellation of memorials across the American South and Midwest that aimed to confront a history of White terrorism against Black Americans. The course drew on such precedents as the Equal Justice Initiative's (EJI) National Memorial for Peace and

Justice, the Black Holocaust Museum, and 'Reconstructions' exhibit at MOMA, among other sources. Another impetus to the recognized its 1930 lynching of Abe Smith and Thomas Shipp, an act of public violence that inspired the civil rights anthem 'Strange Fruit'. Community members collected soil from outside the Grant County Courthouse, where the lynching happened, to add to the EJI's collection.

After graduates and undergraduate stakeholders worked through the design of an outdoor installation in recognition of the Marion lynching, they thereafter chose a collection of interventions to research and create at other sites. Among such collaborations were a 'Memorial for the Charleston Church Massacre', an installation for 'Remembering the Baltimore Uprising', and a 'Bloody Sunday Memorial pavilion'. Throughout the semester, students conceptualized 'site' as a process of deconstructing different records of racial oppression in various media: printed matter, illustration and photography, or film and social media. The interventions proposed all linked together through an evolving design practice. One critical common bond between them was that students created and deployed a variation of a deconstructivist typographic graffiti to generate each design iteration. Like the street art, this deconstructivist typographic graffiti sought to 'violate boundaries, either implicit or contextual'—whether that meant appearing on the lynching site of the Marian County Court House, or at the foothold of the Edmund Pettus Bridge forever associated with Bloody Sunday (Figure 3.5).[61]

They did so with an aim to induce social critique, to spur the sociological imagination, and to drive the architectural design process alongside their stakeholders. At the semester's close, each graduate student developed a brochure that spoke of the 'experiential agenda' of each intervention created. They reflected on how the designs aimed to preserve the historical memory of the site. The brochures told the counterstories of what visitors might hear, see, smell, touch, taste, take away, or leave behind. They commented on how the experience of the place might change throughout the seasons and during different times of the day. Moreover, the brochures commented on how the creative process aimed to produce an enigmatic architecture that would draw people in and speak to the real memories of the place. They offered aspirations for how the designed experiences and activities on site might be transformative for the users and community generally. Students reflected how the design-research prompts enabled them to acquire a higher level of thinking about architecture and race, and to take an active role in situating the profession in a position of social responsibility, as opposed to silence.

Figure 3.5 The 'Bloody Sunday Memorial' by J. Canaday, B. Williams, and D. Yao; 'Memorial for the Charleston Church Massacre' by N. Conley and N. Porter; and 'Remembering the Baltimore Uprising' by J. Daniyam, A. Strayer, and B. Williams.

Conclusion

As a consequence of the pandemic, instructors created virtual studio environments and design challenges that frequently neglected the physical complexities of site as an absolute material space. Students were at times left in trepidation when unable to visit the site as a physical locale to begin field studies, as they are often engrained with the notion to deem site as a sacred environment. This work explored how the pandemic offered designers an alternative prospect to investigate alternate, and at times inaccessible, conceptions of site. They were prompted to consider it as a series of constraints and opportunities, rather than a proscribed destination. It contrasted absolute and normative notions of site, ground, object, and topography with new ideas about engendering site.

Prior to the pandemic, students incorporated various strategic procedures to develop an alternative construct of site towards generating a response to an inherited architectural artefact. They were asked to reconsider the qualitative properties of the object—its creation, influence, and/or destruction, and its situated awareness among an accessible and physical landscape. During the pandemic, emphasis was placed on the invention of site as different media and/or an evolutionary body as a means to explore its many implicit and explicit qualities.

Effectively, this chapter argues that alternative media may serve as a surrogate site, whether physical, imaginary, or generate, the nature of which may unfold into a new virtual paradigm. The argument herein is that an inaccessible absolute physical site is of less concern than a complex alternate material or tangible site, which makes itself immediately available to students during the pandemic.

Notes

1 David Harvey, *Spaces of Global Capitalism* (London: Verso, 2006), 143.
2 Pier Vittorio Aureli, *The Possibility of an Absolute Architecture* (Cambridge: MIT Press, 2011), ix.
3 Patrik Schumacher, *The Autopoiesis of Architecture*, 2 vols., vol. I (London: Wiley & Sons, 2011), 89; Nathaniel Coleman, "The Myth of Autonomy," *Architecture Philosophy* 1, no. 2 (2015).
4 Graham Harman, *Object-Oriented Ontology: A New Theory of Everything* (London: Penguin, 2018); Charles Jencks, *The Story of Post-Modernism: Five Decades of the Ironic, Iconic and Critical in Architecture* (London: Wiley, 2011).
5 Colin Rowe and Fred Koetter, *Collage City* (Cambridge: MIT, 1983), 2–84.

6. Ilka Ruby and Andreas Ruby, *Groundscapes. The Re-Discovery of the Ground in Contemporary Architecture* (Barcelona: Gustavo Gili, 2006), 24.
7. Michael Hensel, *Grounds and Envelopes* (New York: Routledge, 2015), 23.
8. John Rajchman, *Constructions* (Cambridge: MIT Press, Constructions), 77–8.
9. David Leatherbarrow, *Uncommon Ground: Architecture, Technology, and Topography* (Cambridge: MIT Press, 2000), ix.
10. Greg Lynn, *Folds, Bodies, & Blobs: Collected Essays* (Bruxelles: La Lettre Volée, 1998), 105–6.
11. Grahame Shane, "The Emergence of Landcape Urbanism," in *The Landscape Urbanism Reader*, ed. Charles Waldheim (New York: Princeton Architectural Press, 2006), 56–68; Georgia Daskalakis, Charles Waldheim, and Jason Young, eds., *Stalking Detroit* (London: Actar, 2001).
12. Ruby and Ruby, *Groundscapes. The Re-Discovery of the Ground in Contemporary Architecture*, 24–9.
13. Edouard Glissant, *Caribbean Discourse: Selected Essays*, trans. J. Michael Dash (Charlottesville: University Press of Virginia, 1996), 150.
14. Gevork Hartoonian, *Architecture and Spectacle: A Critique* (Farnham: Ashgate, 2012), 38.
15. Gevork Hartoonian, *The Crisis of the Object: The Architecture of Theatricality* (New York: Routledge, 2006), 31.
16. Marc Augé, *Non-Places: an Introduction to Supermodernity* (London: Verso, 2008), viii.
17. Jean Baudrillard, *The Consumer Society: Myths and Structures* (London: Ssage, 1998); Guy Debord, *The Society of the Spectacle* (Detroit: Black & Red, 1970); Herbert Marcuse, *One-Dimensional Man: Studies in the Ideology of Advanced Industrial Society* (New York: Routledge, 1964). Take for, instance, the city map of Dubai that was widely distributed to tourists arriving at the Dubai International Airport in the mid to late 2000s. It featured more so a vision for the Palm Jebel Ali, and other yet to be completed projects, than reality. Rather than taking tourists to such places, cab drivers would pled ignorance and instead drop tourists off at the mall.
18. William J. Mitchell, *e-topia: Urban Life, Jim—But Not As We Know It* (Cambridge: MIT Press, 2000).
19. Theodor Adorno, *Negative Dialectics* (London: Routledge, 1973).
20. William J.R. Curtis, *Modern Architecture Since 1900* (London: Phaidon, 2013).
21. Leatherbarrow, *Uncommon Ground: Architecture, Technology, and Topography*, ix.
22. Harvey, *Spaces of Global Capitalism*, 143; Rajchman, *Constructions*, 77–8.
23. David Leatherbarrow, *Topographical Stories, Studies in Landscape and Architecture* (Philadelphia: University of Pennsylvania Press, 2004), 251–4.
24. Vittorio Gregotti, "Address to the New York Architectural League, October 1982," Section A1, no. 1 (Feb/March 1983): 8, 17.

25 Mark Smout, Laura Allen, *Augmented landscapes* (New York: Princeton Architectural Press, 2007), 6–9.
26 Smout, Allen, *Augmented Landscapes*, 6–9.
27 Bernard Cache and Jean Wilcox, *Earth Moves the Furnishing of Territories* (Cambridge: MIT Press, 1995), 10.
28 El-Setouhy, Hamdy, "Future Heritage: UIA's Responsibility" in *UIA 2021 RIO: 27th World Congress of Architects.* (Washington D.C.: ACSA, 2021), 1203–4.
29 Gottfried Semper and Harry Francis Mallgrave, *Style: Style in the Technical and Tectonic Arts; or, Practical Aesthetics* (Los Angeles: Getty Research Inst., 2004), 725–51.
30 Semper and Mallgrave, *Style: Style in the Technical and Tectonic Arts; or, Practical Aesthetics* (Los Angeles: Getty Research Inst., 2004), 725–51.
31 González and D'Acunto, "Short Stereotomic Models in Architecture." 177–84; Robin Evans, *The Projective Cast: Architecture and Its Three Geometries* (Cambridge: MIT Press, 1995), 179–80.
32 Lars Spuybroek, *The Architecture of Continuity* (Rotterdam: NAi, 2008), 25.
33 Tim Ingold, *Lines: A Brief History* (New York: Routledge, 2007), 39–47.
34 Tim Ingold, *The Life of Lines* (New York: Routledge, 2015), 13–7.
35 Jean-François Lyotard, *The Postmodern Condition: A Report on Knowledge*, trans. Geoff Bennington and Brian Massumi (Minneapolis: University of Minnesota Press, 1984).
36 Owen Hopkins, "Postmodernism Revisited," in *The Return of the Past*, ed. Owen Hopkins and Erin McKeller (London: Sir John Soane's Museum, 2018).
37 Charles Jencks, "Contextual Counterpoint," *Architectural Design: Radical Post-Modernism* 81, no. 5 (2011): 61–7; Jencks, *The Story of Post-Modernism: Five Decades of the Ironic, Iconic and Critical in Architecture.*
38 Terry Farrell and Adam Nathaniel Furman, *Revisiting Postmodernism* (London: RIBA, 2017).
39 Kate Nesbitt, ed., *Theorizing a New Agenda For Architecture* (New York: Princeton Architectural Press, 1996), 16–71.
40 Charles Jencks, *Modern Movements in Architecture* (London: Penguin Books, 1985).
41 Jencks, *The Story of Post-Modernism: Five Decades of the Ironic, Iconic and Critical in Architecture*, 30.
42 Tim Ingold, *The Perception of the Environment: Essays on Livelihood, Dwelling and Skill* (New York: Routledge, 2000), 77.
43 Lebbeus Woods, *Radical Reconstruction* (New York: Princeton Architectural Press, 1997); David Harvey, *Spaces of Hope* (Edinburgh: Edinburgh University Press, 2000); Ruth Levitas, *The Concept of Utopia* (Oxford: Peter Lang, 2011).
44 Sam Griffiths, Charles Holland, and Sam Jacob, "A Field Guide to Radical Post-Modernism," *Architectural Design: Radical Post-Modernism* 81, no. 05 (2011), 46–61.
45 Coleman, "The Myth of Autonomy," 172.
46 Henri Bergson, *Creative Evolution*, trans. Arthur Mitchell (New York: Holt and Company, 1913), 272.

47 Denis Diderot, *Rameau's Nephew and Other Works* (Cambridge: Hackett, 1976), 92.
48 Lars Spuybroek, *The Sympathy of Things, Ruskin and the Ecology of Design* (The Netherlands: V2_NAI Publishing, 2011), 7–10.
49 Jane Rendell, *Site-writing: The Architecture of Art Criticism* (London: Bloomsbury Academic, 2010); Neil Spiller, *Visionary Architecture: Blueprints of the Modern Imagination* (London: Thames & Hudson, 2007).
50 Jean-Paul Sartre, *Huis Clos suivi de Les mouches* (Paris: Éditions Gallimard, 1947), 93.
51 Glissant, *Caribbean Discourse: Selected Essays*, 150.
52 Walter Hood and Grace Mitchell Tada, *Black Landscapes Matter* (Charlottesville: University of Virginia Press, 2020), 2.
53 Robert Bullard, *Dumping in Dixie* (Boulder: Westview Press, 1990); Richard Rothstein, *The Color of Law* (New York: Liveright, 2018). Johnathan Kozol, *Savage Inequalities Children in America's Schools* (New York: Broadway, 1991); Sarah Schindler, "Architectural Exclusion: Discrimination and Segregation Through Physical Design of the Built Environment," *Yale Law Review* 124, no. 6 (2015); N.A., "EQUAL PROTECTION: Is There a Constitutional Right to a Sewer? – Hawkins v. Town of Shaw," *Maryland Law Review* 32, no. 1 (1972).
54 Darell Wayne Fields, *Architecture in Black* (London: Bloomsbury, 2016), 4–43.
55 Kimberlé Crenshaw, "Race, Reform, and Retrenchment: Transformation and Legitimation in Antidiscrimination Law," *Harvard Law Review* 101, no. 7 (1988): 1379; Anthony E. Cook, "Beyond Critical Legal Studies: The Reconstructive Theology of Dr. Martin Luther King, Jr.," *Harvard Law Review* 103, no. 5 (1990): 1044; Gary Peller, "Race-Consciousness," *Duke Law Journal* 39, no. 4 (1990): 760, 70–86.
56 "STOP political correctness in architecture," Facebook, updated 17 March, 2014, accessed 2014, https://www.facebook.com/patrik.schumacher.10/posts/10202631928712343; Peter Eisenman, "Post-Functionalism," in *Theorizing a New Agenda For Architecture*, ed. Kate Nesbitt (Princeton Architectural Press, 1996); M. Speaks, "After Theory," *Architectural Record* 193, no. 6 (2005); Anna Winston, "'Architecture is not art' says Patrik Schumacher in Venice Architecture Biennale rant," *Dezeen* (18 March 2014), https://www.dezeen.com/2014/03/18/architecture-not-art-patrik-schumacher-venice-architecturebiennale-rant/.
57 "'Toward a New GSD'—A Letter from Dean Sarah M. Whiting," Harvard University Graduate School of Design, 2020, accessed 14 June, 2020, https://www.gsd.harvard.edu/2020/06/toward-a-new-gsd-a-letter-from-dean-sarah-m-whiting/. "Black Lives Matter," Yale School of Architecture, 2020, accessed 11 June, 2020, https://www.architecture.yale.edu/news/black-lives-matter. "Hearing the Call for Structural Change," Princeton University School of Architecture, 2020, accessed 7 June, 2020.
58 Sean Anderson and Mabel O. Wilson, eds., *Reconstructions: Architecture and Blackness in America* (New York: Museum of Modern Art, 2021); Irene Cheng, Charles L. Davis II, and Mabel O. Wilson, eds.,

Race and Modern Architecture (Pittsburgh: University of Pittsburgh Press, 2020); Mario Gooden, Dark Space (New York: Columbia 2016); Craig Wilkins, The Aesthetics of Equality (Minneapolis: University of Minnesota Press, 2007).
59   Rodney D. Coates, Abby L. Ferber, and David L. Brunsma, The Matrix of Race: Social Construction, Intersectionality, and Inequality (Los Angeles: Sage, 2017), 22–44; Paul Kivel, Uprooting Racism: How White People Can Work for Racial Justice (Philadelphia: New Society, 2011).
60   Matthew Desmond and Mustafa Emirbayer, Racial Domination, Racial Progress: the Sociology of Race in America (New York: McGraw-Hill, 2010), 51.
61   Sekou Cooke, Hip-Hop Architecture (London: Bloomsbury, 2021), 164–5.

Bibliography

Adorno, Theodor. *Negative Dialectics*. London: Routledge, 1973.

Anderson, Sean, and Mabel O. Wilson, eds. *Reconstructions: Architecture and Blackness in America*. New York: Museum of Modern Art, 2021.

Augé, Marc. *Non-Places: An Introduction to Supermodernity*. London: Verso, 2008.

Aureli, Pier V. *The Possibility of an Absolute Architecture*. Cambridge: MIT Press, 2011.

Baudrillard, Jean. *The Consumer Society: Myths and Structures*. London: Sage, 1998.

Bergson, Henri. *Creative Evolution*. Translated by Arthur Mitchell. New York: Holt and Company, 1913.

Deborah Berke, FAIA LEED AP, *Black Lives Matter*. Yale School of Architecture, 2020, accessed 11 June, 2020, https://www.architecture.yale.edu/news/black-lives-matter.

Bullard, Robert. *Dumping in Dixie*. Boulder: Westview Press, 1990.

Cache, Bernard, and Jean Wilcox. *Earth Moves the Furnishing of Territories*. Cambridge: MIT Press, 1995.

Castellón, González Juan José, and Pierluigi D'Acunto. "Stereotomic Models in Architecture." CAADence in Architecture Conference Proceedings, Budapest, 2016.

Cheng, Irene, Charles L. Davis II, and Mabel O. Wilson, eds. *Race and Modern Architecture*. Pittsburgh: University of Pittsburgh Press, 2020.

Coates, Rodney D., Abby L. Ferber, and David L. Brunsma. *The Matrix of Race: Social Construction, Intersectionality, and Inequality*. Los Angeles: Sage, 2017.

Coleman, Nathaniel. "The Myth of Autonomy." *Architecture Philosophy* 1, no. 2 (2015): 157–78.

Cook, Anthony E. "Beyond Critical Legal Studies: The Reconstructive Theology of Dr. Martin Luther King, Jr." *Harvard Law Review* 103, no. 5 (1990): 985–1044.

Cooke, Sekou. *Hip-Hop Architecture*. London: Bloomsbury, 2021.

Crenshaw, Kimberlé. "Race, Reform, and Retrenchment: Transformation and Legitimation in Antidiscrimination Law." *Harvard Law Review* 101, no. 7 (1988): 1331–87.
Curtis, William J.R. *Modern Architecture since 1900*. London: Phaidon, 2013.
Daskalakis, Georgia, Charles Waldheim, and Jason Young, eds. *Stalking Detroit*. London: Actar, 2001.
Debord, Guy. *The Society of the Spectacle*. Detroit: Black & Red, 1970.
Desmond, Matthew, and Mustafa Emirbayer. *Racial Domination, Racial Progress: The Sociology of Race in America*. New York: McGraw-Hill, 2010.
Diderot, Denis. *Rameau's Nephew and Other Works*. Cambridge: Hackett, 1976.
Eisenman, Peter. "Post-Functionalism." In *Theorizing a New Agenda for Architecture*, edited by Kate Nesbitt, 78–83. New York: Princeton Architectural Press, 1996.
El-Setouhy, Hamdy, "Future Heritage: UIA's Responsibility." In *UIA 2021 RIO: 27th World Congress of Architects*, 1203–4. Washington D.C.: ACSA, 2021.
Evans, Robin. *The Projective Cast: Architecture and Its Three Geometries*. Cambridge: MIT Press, 1995.
Farrell, Terry, and Adam N. Furman. *Revisiting Postmodernism*. London: RIBA, 2017.
Fields, Darell W. *Architecture in Black*. London: Bloomsbury, 2016.
Glissant, Edouard. *Caribbean Discourse: Selected Essays*. Translated by J. Michael Dash. Charlottesville: University Press of Virginia, 1996.
Gooden, Mario. *Dark Space*. New York: Columbia, 2016.
Gregotti, Vittorio. "Address to the New York Architectural League, October 1982." Section A1, no. 1 (Feb/March 1983).
Griffiths, Sam, Charles Holland, and Sam Jacob. "A Field Guide to Radical Post-Modernism." *Architectural Design: Radical Post-Modernism* 81, no. 05 (2011): 46–61.
Harman, Graham. *Object-Oriented Ontology: A New Theory of Everything*. London: Penguin, 2018.
Hartoonian, Gevork. *Architecture and Spectacle: A Critique*. Farnham: Ashgate, 2012.
———. *The Crisis of the Object: The Architecture of Theatricality*. New York: Routledge, 2006.
Harvey, David. *Spaces of Global Capitalism*. London: Verso, 2006.
———. *Spaces of Hope*. Edinburgh: Edinburgh University Press, 2000.
Hensel, Michael. *Grounds and Envelopes*. New York: Routledge, 2015.
Hood, Walter, and Grace M. Tada. *Black Landscapes Matter*. Charlottesville: University of Virginia Press, 2020.
Hopkins, Owen. "Postmodernism Revisited." In *The Return of the Past*, edited by Owen Hopkins and Erin McKeller. London: Sir John Soane's Museum, 2018.
Ingold, Tim. *The Life of Lines*. New York: Routledge, 2015.
———. *Lines: A Brief History*. New York: Routledge, 2007.
———. *The Perception of the Environment: Essays on Livelihood, Dwelling and Skill*. New York: Routledge, 2000.

Jencks, Charles. "Contextual Counterpoint." *Architectural Design: Radical Post-Modernism* 81, no. 5 (2011): 61–7.

———. *Modern Movements in Architecture*. London: Penguin Books, 1985.

———. *The Story of Post-Modernism: Five Decades of the Ironic, Iconic and Critical in Architecture*. London: Wiley, 2011.

Kivel, Paul. *Uprooting Racism: How White People Can Work for Racial Justice*. Philadelphia: New Society, 2011.

Kozol, Johnathan. *Savage Inequalities Children in America's Schools*. New York: Broadway, 1991.

Leatherbarrow, David. *Topographical Stories, Studies in Landscape and Architecture*. Philadelphia: University of Pennsylvania Press, 2004.

———. *Uncommon Ground: Architecture, Technology, and Topography*. Cambridge: MIT Press, 2000.

Levitas, Ruth. *The Concept of Utopia*. Oxford: Peter Lang, 2011.

Lynn, Greg. *Folds, Bodies, & Blobs: Collected Essays*. Bruxelles: La Lettre Volée, 1998.

Lyotard, Jean-François. *The Postmodern Condition: A Report on Knowledge*. Translated by Geoff Bennington and Brian Massumi. Minneapolis: University of Minnesota Press, 1984.

Marcuse, Herbert. *One-Dimensional Man: Studies in the Ideology of Advanced Industrial Society*. New York: Routledge, 1964.

Mitchell, William J. *E-Topia: Urban Life, Jim—But Not as We Know It*. Cambridge: MIT Press, 2000.

N.A. "Equal Protection: Is There a Constitutional Right to a Sewer? – Hawkins V. Town of Shaw." *Maryland Law Review* 32, no. 1 (1972): 70–86.

Nesbitt, Kate, ed. *Theorizing a New Agenda for Architecture*. New York: Princeton Architectural Press, 1996.

Peller, Gary. "Race-Consciousness." *Duke Law Journal* 39, no. 4 (1990). 758–847.

Monica Ponce de Leon Hearing the Call for Structural Change. Princeton University School of Architecture, 2020, accessed 7 June, 2020. https://soa.princeton.edu/content/Hearing-the-Call-for-Structural-Change

Rajchman, John. *Constructions*. Cambridge: MIT Press, Constructions.

Rendell, Jane. *Site-Writing: The Architecture of Art Criticism*. London: Bloomsbury Academic, 2010.

Rothstein, Richard. *The Color of Law*. New York: Liveright, 2018.

Rowe, Colin, and Fred Koetter. *Collage City*. Cambridge: MIT, 1983.

Ruby, Ilka, and Andreas Ruby. *Groundscapes. The Re-Discovery of the Ground in Contemporary Architecture*. Barcelona: Gustavo Gili, 2006.

Sartre, Jean-Paul *Huis Clos Suivi De Les Mouches*. Paris: Éditions Gallimard, 1947.

Schindler, Sarah. "Architectural Exclusion: Discrimination and Segregation through Physical Design of the Built Environment." *Yale Law Review* 124, no. 6 (2015): 1836–2201.

Schumacher, Patrik. *The Autopoiesis of Architecture. 2 vols*. Vol. I, London: Wiley & Sons, 2011.

Patrik Schumacher "Stop Political Correctness in Architecture." Facebook, Updated 17 March, 2014, accessed 2014, https://www.facebook.com/patrik.schumacher.10/posts/10202631928712343.

Semper, Gottfried, and Harry Francis Mallgrave. *Style: Style in the Technical and Tectonic Arts; or, Practical Aesthetics*. Los Angeles: Getty Research Inst., 2004.

Shane, Grahame. "The Emergence of Landcape Urbanism." In *The Landscape Urbanism Reader*, edited by Charles Waldheim, 56–68. New York: Princeton Architectural Press, 2006.

Smout, Mark, Laura Allen. *Augmented Landscapes*. New York: Princeton Architectural Press, 2007.

Speaks, M. "After Theory." *Architectural Record* 193, no. 6 (2005): 72–3.

Spiller, Neil. *Visionary Architecture: Blueprints of the Modern Imagination*. London: Thames & Hudson, 2007.

Spuybroek, Lars. *The Architecture of Continuity*. Rotterdam: NAi, 2008.

———. *The Sympathy of Things, Ruskin and the Ecology of Design*. The Netherlands: V2_NAI Publishing, 2011.

Sarah M. Whiting, "'Toward a New Gsd'—a Letter from Dean Sarah M. Whiting." Harvard University Graduate School of Design, 2020, accessed 14 June, 2020, https://www.gsd.harvard.edu/2020/06/toward-a-new-gsd-a-letter-from-dean-sarah-m-whiting/.

Wilkins, Craig. *The Aesthetics of Equality*. Minneapolis: University of Minnesota Press, 2007.

Winston, Anna. "'Architecture Is Not Art' Says Patrik Schumacher in Venice Architecture Biennale Rant." *Dezeen* (18 March 2014). https://www.dezeen.com/2014/03/18/architecture-not-art-patrik-schumacher-venice-architecturebiennale-rant/.

Woods, Lebbeus. *Radical Reconstruction*. New York: Princeton Architectural Press, 1997.

4 Sensorial Strategies

A Phenomenological Approach Connecting Site to Interior Design

Lisa Phillips

Introduction

Informed design begins with research and analysis of various factors that can potentially impact a final project. Programmatic requirements, regional and historical contexts, and existing physical parameters must all be evaluated. When considering physical studies, architects tend to examine distinguishing features in the landscape and nearby buildings for inspiration. By contrast, interior designers typically seek a more focused approach, surveying internal contexts within the building envelope. Designers often consider elements that can be reused and materials that can be adapted. Might current proportions be maintained? Are there building inconsistencies that can be embellished upon? Such analysis is integral to the interior design process, particularly in the pre-design and schematic design phases. Understanding the site thoroughly enables designers to clearly identify what elements can be utilized to establish the mood that the end user should perceive. Whether it be an atmosphere of peace, collaboration, or one that promotes activity or creativity, understanding the existing context can often support and elevate project goals.

Although studies of the internal envelope are valuable, they have their limitations as well. While successful designs can certainly be inward focused, choosing to deny views of the exterior or even natural light to accomplish a specific effect, many projects do not share this concept and may benefit by continuing analysis beyond the boundaries of the building shell. Though many instinctive designers capably form relationships between interior and exterior, they often do so primarily through visual connections, rather than considering the advantages of multisensory stimuli in the exterior environment and how these have the potential to transform interior solutions. Before a user even crosses

DOI: 10.4324/9781003322726-5

the threshold, she has collected sensory data from her approach. No one arrives a neutral vessel; they are a product of the corporeal information they have collected from their journey. Did she arrive via a busy urban thoroughfare or a quiet country path? What were the surfaces under her feet during her approach? The smells leading up to the entry? The views, both good and bad? What sounds filled her ears? Once the threshold is crossed to the interior of the building, does this connection to the exterior cease to exist, or is it possible to maintain and even enhance it?

Exterior inspired multisensory design has the ability to connect deeply to users, linking to both hearts and memories. It is these spaces that anticipate one's needs, both physical and emotional, that are the most enduring. Consider the aroma and warmth of embers in the fireplace after coming in from the cold, the sound and light mist of running water on a humid day, shadows after bright sunlight, or smoothness after natural textures. It may be bold moves that delight and connect users to form, but often it is the consideration of subtle sensory details, such as understated contrasts, that make the greatest impact. When an overall experience is formed between the outdoors and indoors, a more comprehensive narrative is built by the designer. In order to consider these possibilities, however, a thorough analysis of the surrounding site must be conducted, seeking opportunities to create these multisensory exterior-inspired settings.

Context

Interior design has long been connected with the exterior environment, particularly in the research of biophilic principles that emphasize the strong connection individuals have to the natural world. Humans have an innate attraction to water, for example, and any contact with water, whether visual, aural, or tactile, is desirable to interior users.[1] Natural ventilation is another essential aspect of biophilia, one with the potential to provide pleasant smells, changes in temperature and humidity, as well as the welcoming sensation of air movement across skin.[2] Additional biophilic strategies that interior designers utilize include incorporating plantings or using natural materials like wood or stone to engage a user's tactile senses, all techniques that engage a visitor fully in the built environment.

Designing for the senses is also not a new idea. This concept is woven into many aspects of both architecture and interior design throughout history, but it has seen a significant resurgence in the design community in recent years. With his book, *Phenomenology of Perception,* originally published in 1945, philosopher Maurice Merleau-Ponty was one of the forerunners of related modern discussions. His work focuses primarily on how humans perceive the world, suggesting that we have a complex method of dealing with our physical environs and that our full range of senses are what help us to understand the situations we are presented with. His theory postulated that humans view spaces as incomplete, anonymous, and not fully formed; however, there is more to perceive beyond what one views, "...and not merely more visible being, but also more tangible or audible being...a depth of the object that no sensory withdrawal will ever fully exhaust."[3] He goes on to explain that to understand "the intention" of what we experience, we use our bodies to make sense of it; they are the "accord between what we aim at and what is given, between the intention and the realization—and the body is our anchorage in (this) world."[4] In short, our environments are ours to make of as we will, to discern through experience and discovery, and our senses aid us in these processes. Each user may have a slightly different outcome according to how they have immersed themselves in the design and what those encounters mean to them based on past experiences and their own unique perceptions; however, the more opportunities designers have provided, the fuller the expression of each journey.

Merleau-Ponty's work went on to inspire many others in the field after him. Juhani Pallasmaa, a late twentieth-century architect who advocated for an understanding of full sensory stimuli in place making, is one of the most notable of those in the design fields. Although vision has been one of the most prominent human senses, Pallasmaa questions the domination of sight in current architecture, believing it to be the least intimate sense, as it can occur at the greatest distance.[5] This may be one of the reasons that so many of today's spaces fail to connect with their intended users, as they lack multisensory stimulation. It is one thing to view patterns and textures, but something else entirely to run your fingers over roughly hewn wood below you, feeling the warmth of the material as you explore the uneven grain. To deny tactile variations goes against human nature because, as anthropologist Ashley Montagu explains, "...the skin is the largest sensory organ of the body"[6] and the first to become functional in humans. The sense of touch is how users learn about their environment, "by which the external world is perceived."[7] To design for sight primarily denies the full potential of all that a built environment can offer.

With modern spaces often forming such a distinction between exterior and interior, they are also traditionally devoid of natural smells and sounds, yet humans crave these almost instinctually, and if not provided, they often add them back in artificially with candles, incense, or white noise machines. With studies showing that smells and sounds from the outdoors reduce stress,[8] interior designers can take note that external stimuli will be welcome additions to their proposals.

When considering how to weave exterior and interior stimuli, an overall narrative for the design should be taken into account. Multisensory spaces often have what architect Peter Zumthor would describe as an "atmosphere," an unavoidable "first impression of a space," a way of moving the user through with "air, noises, sound, colours, material presences, textures, (temperature, light, and) forms."[9] Juhani Pallasmaa believes that, in fact, these features are comprehended before any other "conscious observation of details"[10] in a design. When working to create atmosphere, one must consider how each area can optimize the senses to create a mood or provoke an emotional response. The resultant designs are intimate and, in many ways, interactive, beckoning to be touched rather than remain at a distance, avoiding the reliance on sight alone.[11] Zumthor discusses the delicate role of materials in creating atmosphere and how their proximity needs to be addressed thoughtfully. If at too far of a distance from each other, they may not provide the desired effect. Additionally, they may not work together well if too near one another.[12] Every decision in a project must be considered from the user's experience.

Zumthor's project, Therme Vals[13] (Figure 4.1), is a famous example of a multisensory design capable of evoking raw and poignant responses. This design for a hotel and spa in Switzerland is perched over local quartzite slabs that dominate the project and contrast with the surrounding green mountainside. These slabs are the primary material for both the exterior and interior walls, blurring the distinction between the two. A vital aspect of Peter Zumthor's ideas about atmosphere is that it emphasizes the "tension between interior and exterior" and requires consideration be given to the thresholds between them.[14] These tenuous thresholds allow visitors to pass back and forth between the outdoor and interior pools throughout their stay. Outside, the smells and sounds of the environments and the sensations of the natural elements can be taken in in their entirety, with the Swiss countryside providing a full range of stimuli. Respite can be found in exploring smaller bathing areas adjacent to the main open-air pool or by moving to the interior. There are warm pools, cold pools, spaces with specific colors to enhance the experience, and areas where visitors can drink the water, evoking the sense of taste. Moreover, of course,

Sensorial Strategies 83

Figure 4.1 Therme Vals in Switzerland by architect, Peter Zumthor. Photo by lauravr/Shutterstock.com.

the sound of moving water is always present, making the encounter a true multisensory affair. Therme Vals is a considerable example of inclusive design, with exterior stimuli informing the interior, including the textures and temperature of natural materials, and the play of light, shadow, and steam working together to produce a setting of peace and tranquility. Zumthor's goal for the project, to "seduce" the user, clearly comes across throughout, allowing visitors to find their own path through the design rather than guiding them and enabling them to "form their own attachments." He calls it a "voyage of discovery," where guests are invited to explore.[15] This project serves as an excellent multisensory case study, showing how the built environment is able to convey an immersive and emotional experience and how this is achieved by taking advantage of exterior sensory stimuli.

The Proposal

With these principles and theories in mind, an experiment was undertaken to determine if analyzing exterior environments might better inform interior design students and enable them to produce richer multisensory interior solutions. In fall 2020 and 2021, this pedagogical experiment was conducted with two separate groups of junior interior design students at Thomas Jefferson University in Philadelphia, the sixth largest city in the United States. This intensive upper-level studio met for 11 hours a week, providing sufficient time for a thorough investigative process. The two groups together totaled 30 students, 29 female and 1 male. The ages ranged from 20 to 25 years old, with most on the younger end of this spectrum.

As a five-week design problem, students were tasked with designing a tranquility pod. This typology was inspired by our society's increasing need for temporary removal from stressful environments. In 2018, Americans reported feeling the highest level of stress in a decade, according to an annual Gallup poll.[16] Chronic stress disrupts nearly every system in the human body, including our immune system, heart, and memory, and it has been known to speed up the aging process and cause heart disease and diabetes.[17] Tranquility pods have the ability to alleviate stress by providing a much-needed opportunity for users to obtain distance from the tensions in their daily life, allowing them a unique means to re-center.

The pod itself was a prefabricated box of approximately 15′×15′×15′—although this size could be expanded if the proposed program justified it. The project brief had few limitations, only noting that the design should focus on addressing stress relief in whatever form was appropriate for the user group. This might involve one singular activity or several activities. Students were able to add doors, windows, and skylights as needed.

The Process

For most students, this project was their first experience designing for stress alleviation and considering senses in depth in their work. As a result, extensive discussions and lectures were conducted before designing began. Students were assigned readings from Juhani Pallasmaa's *The Eyes of the Skin*.[18] Other early conversations included sharing examples of spaces utilized for stress alleviation, meditation,[19] and contemplation. Case studies included Tadao Ando's Meditation Space outside the UNESCO headquarters in Paris,[20] Hil Architects' Meditation Hall in Eastern China,[21] and The Windhover Contemplative Center at Stanford University, designed by Aidlin Darling Design.[22]

Each student selected their own clients from within the local community, choosing a profession that they felt would benefit from utilizing a tranquility pod. They did this by researching groups that are more prone to stressful conditions at work, including long hours, heavy workloads, unrealistic job expectations, and/or dangerous working conditions.[23] Once a group was identified, students investigated the details of the occupation more to learn about their users' schedule and specific work-related physical and mental stresses. Additionally, they were required to interview someone from within the community they chose to provide first-person information about routine, specific stressors, ways that they relieved their tensions, and what they would like to see in a design for tranquility.

The entire group simultaneously researched general methods for combatting stress in the built environment. These included multisensory design considerations, such as smells and sounds that are considered calming. Many natural stimuli were found among the collected information. Scents in this category included basil, lavender, orange, and lemon.[24] Sounds consisted of moving water, crackling fire, and the song of birds.[25] Not surprisingly, textures that reduce stress are also tied to nature, including wood, stone, and fur. A sampling of foods that reduce stress are bananas, strawberries, dark chocolate, pumpkin seeds, almonds, and peanuts, to name but a few.[26]

With initial research completed, the siting of the pods was considered next. Density studies were conducted to locate those who were within the user group. By examining these findings, students identified where the largest concentrations of the occupations they had chosen to create pods for existed. Out of these, they selected one area to focus on for the siting. Sensory map explorations then began in earnest (Figure 4.2). Students were asked to visit their sites when the users would most likely be there, taking into consideration the shifts they worked, breaks they might have, and times they were most likely to be at the pod. They were told to observe physical opportunities as one part of their site analysis—similar to the examinations of sun and wind that are part of a traditional site study—along with positive and negative views, circulation, and vegetation in the area. These aspects of a site are just as significant for an interior designer to understand as they are for an architect. Where are the best views on which they might want to capitalize? In which directions does the sun rise and set? How can views be considered, and how can low sunlight be kept from entering the pod? Is there an area where the winter wind blows that should be kept warm on the interior?

The next set of studies was slightly more unique. Students were asked to create a behavioral analysis in which they examined the activities of the visitors to the site. What areas were utilized or not utilized? Were visitors in the area bringing their children to play? Feeding birds? Exercising or relaxing? Perhaps the area was a place of intense activity at the time of the study? By understanding how the site was currently being used, students could determine the most suitable pod location.

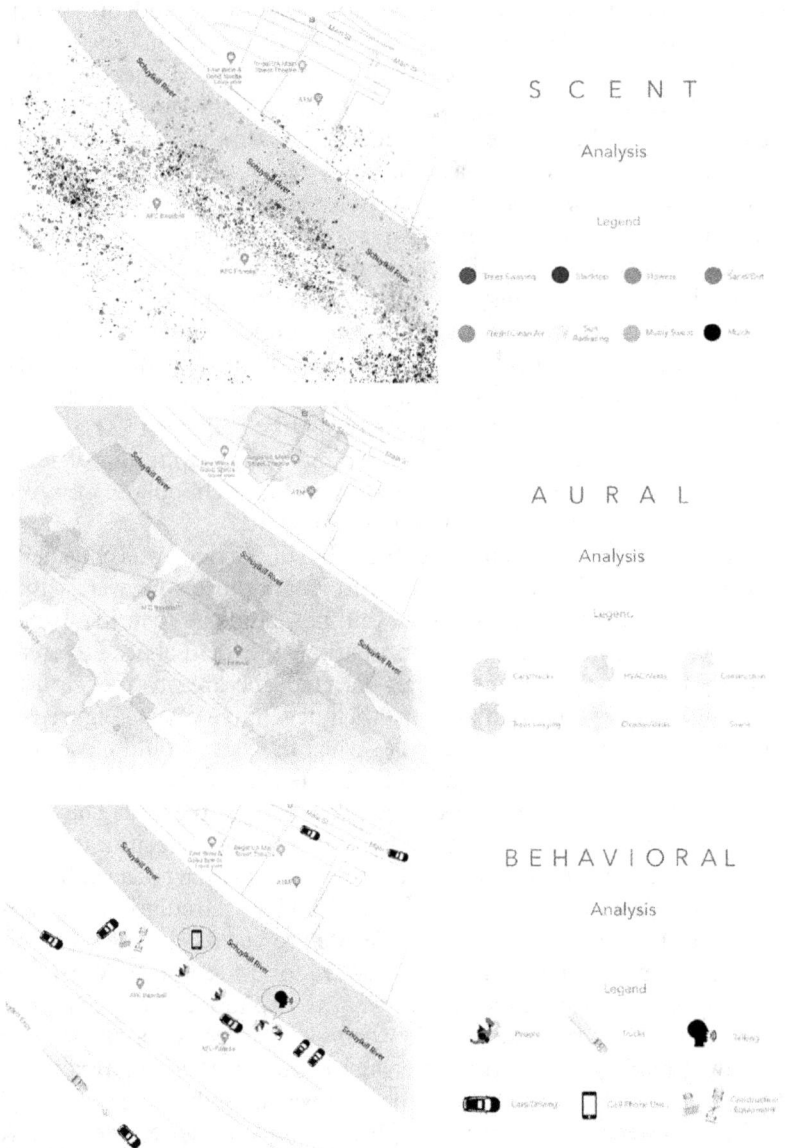

Figure 4.2 Sensory maps created by student, Kaylie Siwy, F'20 term at Thomas Jefferson University.

In addition, from an interior perspective, they could identify any activities that they might want to connect with or stay away from.

Inspired by the work of Kate McLean, a designer and researcher at England's Canterbury Christ Church University who creates Smellscapes,[27] the students also created a scent analysis for their site. The olfactory sense is one that is often overlooked in design; however, it is one of the most intimate senses, and it is more connected with emotions and memory than any other sense. By analyzing the exterior environment, students were able to determine the scents in the air at the site and decide if they were welcoming or not. Because distractions can sometimes make smells harder to isolate, this analysis was conducted while wearing a blindfold to try to block out all other senses except for smell. Students were asked to have a partner guide them, while noting what was observed, categorizing the scents, both good and bad, and remarking on the intensity of each smell.

Finally, the class performed a similar walk, also wearing a blindfold, considering auditory input. Sound is a fascinating sense with endless potential. I have a colleague who records odd bits of sounds whenever he travels to new cities, whether it be the call to prayer, the melody of a local street musician, or the whispers of passersby in an unfamiliar language. Although, he is not overly formal about his collection process, my colleague is responding to ideas that are well known to acoustic ecology researcher Raymond Murray Schafer, who believes that sounds personify place. Schafer suggests that, much like smells, sounds can be noted and categorized, creating analyses he has coined "soundscapes."[28] It is not surprising that sound is connected so emphatically with place, since it is actually one of the most sensitive of the senses. Although we do not often ponder the abilities of the olfactory system, our "...ears can detect vibrations a million times less intense than those we can detect through the sense of touch."[29] This sensitivity actually makes the process of analysis more difficult since sounds in nature are rarely one dimensional; they have various tones, pitches, and intensities. In addition, they last for various durations, with some being constant, while others occur with rhythm, having silence between each incidence. For this reason, during the visit to their site, students were encouraged to notice the strength of the sounds, along with the types of sound, in order to accommodate these variations.[30] If negative sounds occurred, they considered siting the pod away from these areas. The potential for a positive auditory connection between the interior and exterior elements was considered as well.

The synthesis of the information collected was utilized to locate the pod's arrangement on the site. Should it be nearby a thoroughfare or sequestered in the trees? At an edge or pushed to the center? This decision would determine the path to the pod from the main areas of sidewalks or parking areas, so it was not taken lightly. What would the visitor's experience be just before arriving at the tranquility pod? Interior designers are not typically involved in the siting of the building, so some leniency was given in this particular exercise. The purpose of the activity was not to train them to be architects or landscape architects, so no time was spent with grading activities or water mitigation, as these were considered out of the realm of an interior design student's purview.

After a site was determined, concept ideations began through sketching, word association, and model building. Sensory integrations were considered during this early phase as well. In these initial stages, the activities were more freeform in nature, with each sense simply listed and solutions for how to bring each into the pods noted below or clustered around the listed sense. In many cases, students included images, but other students sketched their ideas for sensory inclusion. As space planning evolved, the multisensory designs developed as well. The sensory decisions were organized around plans, sections, and perspectives, with notes to communicate intentions.

Three-dimensional software was employed fairly early as a means to develop a visual language for the pods. This allowed the class to create multiple iterations in swift succession and to experiment with light, color, and materiality in the virtual environment. Special attention was paid to how these aspects would affect the sensory experience and atmospheric qualities in order to achieve optimal results, taking into consideration that users are often hyper aware of their environment during times of isolation and introspection.

The class was also able to take advantage of the campus' material library to select physical finishes, in addition to ordering samples. In lieu of a traditional material board, students were asked to produce a sensory box. These vessels were to hold a representation of the senses, and they were not limited to finish materials; instead, they were asked to represent as many sensory aspects of their pod design as possible. Ideas for these immersions were discussed and conceptualized throughout the project, and they were prototyped during the final week of the presentation.

Results/Analysis

The occupations selected for the user groups were diverse and included many that are widely associated with stressful working environments, such as firefighters, nurses, and police officers, while others were perhaps less obvious but equally deserving of stress mediating pods, such as public transportation employees, restaurant staff, social workers, and members of the clergy. For many groups, stress was caused by expected factors, but in several groups, students found that a primary cause of stress was guiding patients or clients out of crises, including poor physical or mental health, unfavorable financial crises, difficulties with the law, relationship issues, or other personal problems. In all of these situations, assisting others caused concern, sadness, and even grief in their work environments that followed them home after hours.

The use of density studies did assist in selecting the pods' locations, and varied settings were proposed. Some students selected small parks or other natural environments, while several others chose locations near bodies of water. However, a handful chose parking lots or abandoned plots in the middle of dense urban environments. Most notably, a pod for social workers was placed on an underdeveloped asphalt area in the city. This lot was actually close to several offices where social workers were employed, while a green space would have been an impractical distance away. It was felt that these workers were even more in need of tranquility because they had little access to biophilia locally, so this site was chosen in a space convenient to them.

Once locations were determined, the designers turned to site analyses. It is fair to say that many students were initially intimidated by the nature of these studies, as the work of an interior designer is generally of an intimate scale, and the size of these considerations was larger. Yet, once the initial concern passed, the actual analyses were quite powerful. This was not surprising, as interior designers are deeply familiar with environmental psychology, and they are extremely astute at understanding human behavior. Although the sensory studies were new to them, the ideas behind them resonated easily, and they were able to develop high-level studies in most cases. When categorizing smells, for instance, although many common scents were featured—like those of asphalt, flowers, fresh air, and mulch—there were also some that were surprising. Students smelled what they could only label as sweetness, the sun, and fresh water. The same can be said of the collected auditory data. Sounds of traffic, sirens, and birds were common, but whispers of the wind, bike gears, insects, and the hum of mechanical systems and machinery in the distance were also noted. These last sounds may not be discernable if one is simply passing through a neighborhood, but they become clearer when lingering in the quiet and taking in the site. Visitors to a tranquility pod would likely be in a restful state, so scents and sounds would be more acute to them, along with their already strong sense of vision.

These studies guided sensory inspirations throughout the design process. For many designers, ideas are manifested in physical extensions outside the pods. Several featured small, enclosed gardens that could be explored, including areas to sit, lie, and swing. Although students were not expected to design the landscape, many made attempts to show consideration for these spaces and used their knowledge of interior environments to inform the elements they included in those areas. A pod designed for customer service workers featured a small working garden, with tools hung on the interior of the space, encouraging visitors to participate in the upkeep of the herbs, vegetables, and flowers that were planted there. These could be brought in and eaten by visitors, activating their sense of taste. At least two pods featured balconies that acted as focal points at the end of interior paths, with daylight leading guests outside to dramatic natural scenes. The gardens all incorporated multiple senses within them: the smells of plants and nature, as well as the textures of benches and rope or fabric swings and grass or stones under bare feet. Some highlighted the sounds of nearby animals, wind blowing through trees or bushes, and wind chimes. In all of these cases, however, the user became immersed in elements from the exterior.

There were various innovative methods to connect exterior and interior as well. In traditional solutions, these connections are often limited. If an operable window is included in a particular location, it may be for thermal consideration or to bring in fresh air, but during this project, students also considered how the singing of birds and the swaying of tree leaves might enter the pod and provide stress mediation. In several cases, when located near water, the sounds of quickly moving streams and rivers and mossy aromas were welcomed in through operable windows and, in one case, through an actual vent in the floor. Students considered feeding and creating habitats for butterflies, dragonflies, bees, and birds to increase wildlife around the pods in order to provide active scenes to view from the interior. Participating in maintaining these was part of the stress mediation process in some cases. Positive aromas from the exterior were also welcomed in, bringing in an array of scents to enrich the interior spaces.

It should be noted that while there was considerable innovation by the end of the project, during the early ideation phase, students struggled to incorporate all of the senses. They often needed to be reminded to include a full range of sensory stimulation, and additional activities needed to be incorporated to this end. It seemed that the senses remained intangible in many ways to some designers, a sign that they need repeat exposure over time to integrate this type of design into their practice. Of all of the project components, the small physical manifestations of the senses (the boxes) seemed to make the experiment most concrete to them, since they had to produce sensory stimuli to be interacted with by others. By the end, many unconventional items were included that would not appear in a typical interior design presentation. Several boxes asked participants to push down on small plots of live grass or interact with water. Students brought tea, coffee, fruit, and candies—all items that would be present in their tranquility pods—to the final critique in their boxes. Many incorporated smells of the outdoors by featuring real plants, herbs, moss, and dirt. Others tried to duplicate the scent of streams or other nearby water sources. Essential oils with citrus, lavender, and eucalyptus scents were featured prominently in the boxes in an attempt to replicate both indoor and outdoor plantings from the designs. Exterior environmental sounds were brought in via clips of general nature sounds, wind chimes, water bubbling in a brook, or birds chirping. These were designed to be heard when a window was ajar or one of the sliding exterior walls was open. The live plants were meant to be touched as well to represent the gardens that the users had access to. Touch was often engaged through the inclusion of physical materials, but other props were included as well. For instance, hand warmers were used for thermal indications, and small fans were provided to imply airflow when outdoor breezes would be welcomed in. Some students added interactive elements, like paints and a paintbrush or a tiny rake and sand, to simulate the kinesthetic activities that would occur in their pods.

The physical sensory boxes illustrated surprising variety, not just in content but also in concept, as students customized the experiences to emphasize their design's emotional mood. Some students developed more literal boxes, as might be expected, while others utilized baskets to hold their collection of sensory objects. Still others used clasped specialty vessels, and then there were some that were vastly more abstract. One came in a mesh bag, while another came in a layered jar, like a dessert trifle. Most elements from the boxes featured instructions for how to interact with them, asking jurors to *squeeze me, push me,* or *put me up to your ear.* Some students chose to reveal these box's contents all at the end of their presentation, and others revealed their interactions slowly, breaking them down individually throughout the critique.

Although many students' projects were exceptional, a few stood out in terms of their integration of exterior analysis into their projects. Two examples are noted here. In the first example (Figure 4.3), the user group was artists, an occupation that might not immediately be associated with stress; however, artists are under pressure in many different ways since they work on commission and have a pressing need

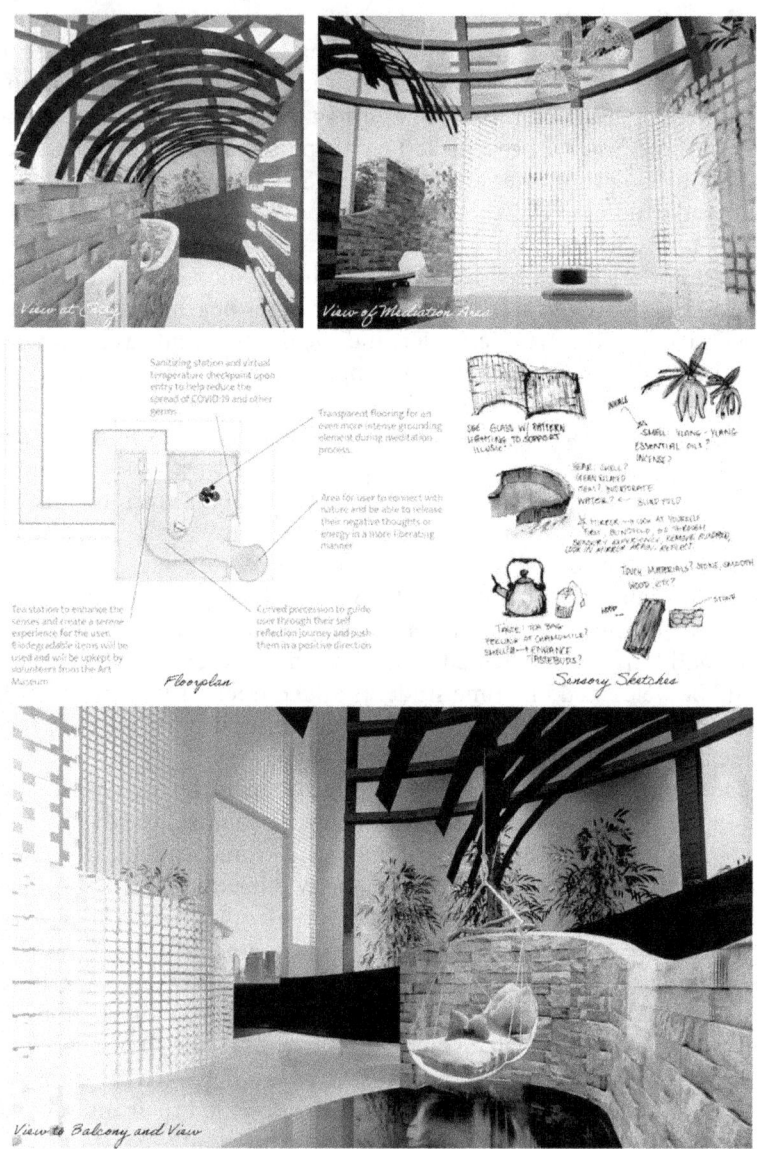

Figure 4.3 Process & final work by student, Charisse Reid, F'20 term at Thomas Jefferson University.

to consistently produce at a high level. Artists often suffer from considerable self-doubt and self-judgment, and they commonly face creative blocks. All of these factors cause a lack of motivation and increase stress levels. Taking this data into consideration, this tranquility pod was not only sited in a natural area to create a refuge of inspiration, but also a place where users could mediate their stress. The student chose a harmonious location in Philadelphia, in the shadow of The Museum of Art, adjacent to Boat House Row and the Schuylkill River. After conducting the site analyses, the student inquired about the prospect of her pod being placed in the river itself, which I allowed, for the sake of the experiment. The design took full advantage of this location, with an entry procession through the landscape moving the user from the exterior into the pod, not via a straight datum, but by way of a twisted route, prolonging the natural views. The interior of the pod was textural, with warm, earth tones that contrasted with the white, clean exterior. To add to this feeling of warmth, a cup of tea was immediately available for visitors to enjoy, triggering the senses of smell and taste upon arrival. Continuing the winding travel around an interior path, rough walls beckoned to be touched, and plants soared overhead to incorporate biophilia. Ylang-Ylang planted within ignited the olfactory sense again with its fruity, floral scent. Near the end of the first curve, a textural wicker swing hung above a glass floor, allowing guests views of the fast-moving water below the pod. Adjacent was a small area for meditation; it featured soft floor cushions surrounded by glass walls. Slick surfaces contrasted with irregular textures in this pod, which incorporated both formal and intimate materials. Users were drawn to a large set of doors that could be left open, allowing the sounds and smells of nature and the water below to flood in on the breezes, inspiring and inviting visitors to step onto the balcony and enjoy the stunning views of The Museum of Art and the Philadelphia skyline. This balanced sensory experience would surely offer a restorative journey to the artists who visited.

Another student designed a tranquility pod for members of the clergy, a group characterized by mental, emotional, and physical fatigue due to a high workload associated with loss, hardship, and suffering (Figure 4.4). After the density study was completed, it was determined that the ideal location for the pod was in a park, near several religious venues. The concept for the project connected to a method of reconnecting spiritually, known as the Sacred Pathways.[31] By including several areas within the pod that featured these pathways, religious leaders could de-stress while experiencing spiritual growth and well-being. Upon entry, the user is greeted by the intellectual area,

94 *Lisa Phillips*

Figure 4.4 Final work by student, Ashley Hurst, F'21 term at Thomas Jefferson University.

Sensorial Strategies 95

where a library and desk area offers space for mindful activities. Wood walls and a stone floor dominate this space, providing a natural, welcoming environment. Just beyond, the student designed a winding hallway lined with plants to lead users to the contemplative space. During warm weather, the breezeblock in this area could be open to the outside so that breezes could flow through, bringing with them the touch of calming winds skimming through the leaves and music of nearby birds. During the analyses, the exterior environment was found to be rich with aromas, including scents of wildflowers, woody pine, and freshly baked bread and coffee, which would also enter through the perforations. In the contemplative space, a small stone bench perched below a circular skylight wraps around the area. From this vantage point, users can focus inward or look upward to watch the movement of clouds, the change of shadows throughout the day, or birds in flight. The creative/worship space is just beyond, where musical instruments are available to play and a sweeping custom wooden bench provides space for lounging and praying. Small windows in this area highlight views of the exterior, while a large window wall welcomes users to extend their visit to a semi-enclosed outdoor garden. In this area, a bench tucked under a generous overhang is provided for visitors to reflect on the plantings, trees, and water feature in the landscape.

These examples illustrate distinct multisensory solutions that connect to the environment through the analysis of the surrounding context. The students' designs displayed innovation and a particular care for users' behavioral patterns above the level of previous studio projects that was both commendable and worth further pursuit in the future.

Assessment

The data collected from the site analyses showed remarkable integration across the two sections. The depth of the interventions, although exceptionally successful in most cases, did vary from student to student. This is natural, given the wide range of occupations in the study. During the interview process, for example, some users suggested the inclusion of sensory deprivation areas since they were so overstimulated during their work days. This resulted in less multisensory incorporation overall in those particular pods. Additionally, since the exterior environments were so wide ranging, it was not surprising that some sites offered more desirable natural sources of external stimulation than others.

During the first year of the project's addition to the studio, most of the senses were utilized without difficulty; however, taste and touch presented some challenges. Although touch is generally easy to consider, it is more difficult to bring in actual elements from the exterior environment, unless they are moved inside—as is the case in wood textures or stone. The other sense that posed a difficulty was taste. Although some students added areas with tea, mints, or chocolates, others were hesitant to add food or drinks, no matter how much the suggestion was made. They struggled even more to think about how they could bring in the tastes of the exterior environment. The student who included the working garden was one of the rare cases who managed to do so successfully. This is not surprising given that in interior design taste is the least consistently utilized of the senses. During the second year of the project, special attention was paid to the sense of taste at the introduction of the project, with recognition that it had been a challenge in the previous iteration. This modification improved its integration during the second year.

During the final critiques, students presented their work to professionals in the field. The multisensory design solutions and physical interactions fascinated the jurors, as they unscrewed caps, squeezed spray bottles, and opened small packages, wondering what sensorial pleasures awaited them. Comments from these jurors, along with instructor observations throughout the term, were utilized in completing a rubric for the project. The relevant criteria on the rubric were as follows: *design considers the community user*, *design engages the senses*, and *sensory interaction was appropriately developed*. The target set for each of the criteria was that at least 85% of the class should score an average grade (3 or better on a scale of 1–5). Ninety percent of the students did manage to score average or better for each criterion, which illustrated that most projects met the target. Moreover, it was noted that the few that did not deliver had failed to conduct enough research in the early stages, leading to reduced design investigation overall. It should be pointed out that incorporation of exterior sensory stimuli was not a stand-alone criterion due to the fact that it was not equally appropriate for all user groups. Instead, it was evaluated within the criteria listed above.

Qualitative feedback was also provided by the jurors, who were intrigued by the enriched sensory projects. The incorporation of exterior sensory studies was applauded, and the sensory stimuli these manifested in the projects were recognized for their innovation. The wide range of solutions was noted, with not only sight, smell, touch, taste, and sound integrations but also kinesthetic and thermal considerations, as many designs featured fire, mist, and fog and took into account temperature and humidity. In addition, through the unique physical sensory vessels, the jurors were able to experience the students' design intentions in an active environment. Their joy echoed throughout the room during their exploration, and they seemed particularly engaged when students revealed the items in the boxes throughout the presentations rather than waiting until the end to go through them. They also appeared to favor the interactions that had expressive instructions, such as the use of strong verbs or sensory words like *scratch me, touch me,* or *inhale deeply!*

Conclusion

Several valuable findings that can be utilized in both the educational setting and the professional interior design setting resulted from this pedagogical experiment.

1 One of the most significant takeaways is that the integrations the students often utilized did require some control over the addition of openings or patios and gardens to connect the interior to the exterior. For these types of analyses to be useful, these design decisions need to fall under the purview of the interior designer, or they need to be a part of the collaborative design process, where designers are able to suggest such potential sensory stimuli into the overall scheme. It is one thing to come equipped with data, but being able to implement it is something else entirely.
2 Exterior sensory analysis can be a powerful tool for interior designers. Through the use of traditional site studies, as well as behavioral, auditory, and scent analyses, a wide range of potential stimuli can be identified and utilized to inform the interior environment.
3 Initial research is key to understanding the many nuances of multisensory design.
4 It takes practice to think beyond the sense of sight when designing. Visual design is a crutch that has become all too common to lean on in the modern world. Considering the full range of senses is a worthwhile exercise, as user groups will benefit from a deeper immersive experience.
5 The physical sensory interactions utilized in this project can easily be adapted to suit most settings. Labeling each sensory interaction with verbs is especially recommended, as these were shown to be particularly effective in drawing the jurors into the experiences.

The insights noted above provided me with valuable understanding of the methodology necessary to incorporate exterior site analysis further within the interior design process. Several adjustments needed to be made along the way to accommodate the skill level of the students and their lack of former knowledge on the topics, but, in the end, these adjustments led to successful work in a majority of projects and examples that can act as case studies for future students. With each year of implementation, new methods are found to improve the outcomes, and it is my hope that the continued usage of exterior analysis will form an excellent skillset that our interior design students will carry with them into their professional lives.

Notes

1. Kausha Modi and Sangramsinh Parmar, "Understanding Biophilia and its Integration with Architecture," *International Journal of Scientific & Engineering Research* 11, no. 5 (May 2020): 1412, https://www.researchgate.net/profile/Sangramsinh-Parmar 2/publication/343190808_Understanding_Biophilia_and_its_integration_with_Architecture/links/5f1b106a92851cd5fa42a12b/Understanding-Biophilia-and-its-integration-with-Architecture.pdf.
2. Ibid 1412
3. Maurice Merleau-Ponty and Colin Smith, *Phenomenology of Perception* (Nevada: Franklin Classics, 2018), 224.
4. Ibid 146.
5. Barbara Erwine, *Creating Sensory Spaces: The Architecture of the Invisible* (New York: Routledge, Taylor & Francis Group, 2017).
6. Ashley Montagu, *Touching: The Human Significance of the Skin* (Memphis, TN: General Books, 2010), 4.
7. Ibid 5
8. Marcus Hedblom et al., "Reduction of Physiological Stress by Urban Green Space in a Multisensory Virtual Experiment," *Scientific Reports* 9, no 1 (2019): 10113, https://www.ncbi.nlm.nih.gov/pmc/articles/PMC6625985/.
9. Peter Zumthor, *Atmospheres: Architectural Environments, Surrounding Objects* (Basel: Birkhäuser Verlag, 2018), 11–17.
10. Juhani Pallasmaa, *The Eyes of the Skin: Architecture and the Senses* (Chichester: Wiley, 2019), 13.
11. Julieanna Preston, *Interior Atmospheres* (Chichester: Wiley, 2008), 5.
12. Ibid 27.
13. Eduardo Souza, "Peter Zumthor's Therme Vals Through the Lens of Fernando Guerra," *ArchDaily*, October 30, 2016, Accessed May 10, 2021, https://www.archdaily.com/798360/peter-zumthors-therme-vals-through-the-lens-of-fernando-guerra.
14. Ibid 45.
15. Zumthor, *Atmospheres*, 41–43.
16. Julie Ray, "Americans' Stress, Worry and Anger Intensified in 2018," *Gallup*, May 4, 2021, Accessed May 5, 2021, https://news.gallup.com/poll/249098/americans-stress-worry-anger-intensified-2018.aspx.

17 Erica Goode, "The Heavy Cost of Chronic Stress," *The New York Times*, December 17, 2002, Accessed May 5, 2021, https://www.nytimes.com/2002/12/17/science/the-heavy-cost-of-chronic-stress.html.
18 Pallasmaa, *The Eyes of the Skin*.
19 Michael Freeman, *Meditative Spaces* (New York: Universe, 2005).
20 Philip Jodidio, in *Ando Complete Works 1975 – Today* (Köln: Taschen, 2016), 140–147.
21 Han Shuang, "Meditation Hall / HIL Architects," *ArchDaily*, February 28, 2019, Accessed May 7, 2021, https://www.archdaily.com/912262/meditation-hall-hil-architects.
22 Lydia Lee, "Windhover Contemplative Center by Aidlin Darling Design," *Architectural Record*, November 6, 2019, Accessed May 7, 2021, https://www.architecturalrecord.com/articles/7993-windhover-contemplative-center-by-aidlin-darling-design.
23 American Psychological Association, "Stress in the Workplace," American Psychological Association, March 2011, Accessed May 10, 2021, https://www.apa.org/news/press/releases/stress/.
24 Akio Nakamura et al., "Stress Repression in Restrained Rats by (R)-(–)-Linalool Inhalation and Gene Expression Profiling of Their Whole Blood Cells," *Journal of Agricultural and Food Chemistry* 57, no. 12 (2009): 5480–5485.
25 Bum-Jin Park et al., "Physiological Effects of Forest Recreation in a Young Conifer Forest in Hinokage Town, Japan," *Silva Fennica* 43, no. 2 (2009): 291–230. Terry Hartig et al., "Tracking Restoration in Natural and Urban Field Settings," *Journal of Environmental Psychology* 23 (2003): 109–123.
Elizabeth Orsega-Smith et al., "Interaction of Stress and Park Use on Psycho-physiological Health in Older Adults," *Journal of Leisure Research* 36, no. 2 (2004): 232–256, https://www.nrpa.org/globalassets/journals/jlr/2004/volume-36/jlr-volume-36-number-2-pp-232-256.pdf. Roger S. Ulrich et al. "Stress Recovery During Exposure to Natural and Urban Environments," *Journal of Environmental Psychology* 11 (1991): 201–230.
26 Cleveland Clinic, "Eat These Foods to Reduce Stress and Anxiety," Cleveland Clinic (June 15, 2021), Accessed April 20, 2022, https://health.clevelandclinic.org/eat-these-foods-to-reduce-stress-and-anxiety/.
27 Kate McLean, "Home," *Sensory Maps*, June 15, 2020, Accessed August 15, 2020, https://sensorymaps.com/.
28 Raymond Murray Schafer, *The Soundscape Our Sonic Environment and the Tuning of the World* (Rochester: Destiny Books, 1993).
29 Massachusetts Institute of Technology. "Mechanism Helps Explain the Ear's Exquisite Sensitivity: A Critical Gel-like Structure in the Inner Ear Moves According to a Ssound's Frequency, Researchers find," *ScienceDaily*, January 16, 2019, Accessed February 1, 2022, www.sciencedaily.com/releases/2019/01/190116110945.htm.
30 Barbara Erwine, *Creating Sensory Spaces: The Architecture of the Invisible* (New York: Routledge, Taylor & Francis Group, 2017), 145.
31 Gary Thomas, *Sacred Pathways: Nine Ways to Connect with God* (Grand Rapids: Zondervan, 2021).

Bibliography

American Psychological Association. "Stress in the Workplace," American Psychological Association, March 2011. https://www.apa.org/news/press/releases/stress/.

Cleveland Clinic. "Eat These Foods to Reduce Stress and Anxiety." Cleveland Clinic. June 14, 2021. Accessed April 20, 2022. https://health.clevelandclinic.org/eat-these-foods-to-reduce-stress-and-anxiety/.

Erwine, Barbara. *Creating Sensory Spaces: The Architecture of the Invisible.* New York: Routledge, Taylor & Francis Group, 2017.

Freeman, Michael. *Meditative Spaces.* New York: Universe, 2005.

Goode, Erica. "The Heavy Cost of Chronic Stress," *The New York Times*, December 17, 2002. Accessed May 5, 2021. https://www.nytimes.com/2002/12/17/science/the-heavy-cost-of-chronic-stress.html.

Hartig, Terry et al. "Tracking Restoration in Natural and Urban Field Settings." *Journal of Environmental Psychology* 23, no. 2 (2003): 109–23. https://doi.org/10.1016/s0272-4944(02)00109-3.

Hedblom, Marcus et al. "Reduction of Physiological Stress by Urban Green Space in a Multisensory Virtual Experiment." *Scientific Reports* 9, 1 (2019): 10113. https://doi.org/10.1038/s41598-019-46099-7.

Jodidio, Philip. Essay. In *Ando Complete Works 1975 – Today*, 140–47. Köln: Taschen, 2016.

Lee, Lydia. "Windhover Contemplative Center by Aidlin Darling Design," *Architectural Record*, November 6, 2019. https://www.architecturalrecord.com/articles/7993-windhover-contemplative-center-by-aidlin-darling-design.

Massachusetts Institute of Technology. "Mechanism Helps Explain the Ear's Exquisite Sensitivity: A Critical Gel-like Structure in the Inner Ear Moves According to a Sound's Frequency, Researchers Find," *ScienceDaily*, January 16, 2019. Accessed February 1, 2022. www.sciencedaily.com/releases/2019/01/190116110945.htm.

McLean, Kate. "Home." *Sensory Maps*, June 15, 2020. https://sensorymaps.com/.

Merleau-Ponty, Maurice, and Colin Smith. *Phenomenology of Perception.* Nevada: Franklin Classics, 2018.

Modi, Kausha, and Sangramsinh Parmar. "Understanding Biophilia and its Integration with Architecture," *International Journal of Scientific & Engineering Research* 11, no. 5 (May 2020). https://www.researchgate.net/profile/Sangramsinh-Parmar-2/publication/343190808_Understanding_Biophilia_and_its_integration_with_Architecture/links/5f1b106a92851cd-5fa42a12b/Understanding-Biophilia-and-its-integration-with-Architecture.pdf.

Montagu, Ashley. *Touching: The Human Significance of the Skin.* Memphis, TN: General Books, 2010.

Nakamura, Akio et al. "Stress Repression in Restrained Rats by (r)-(−)-Linalool Inhalation and Gene Expression Profiling of Their Whole Blood Cells." *Journal of Agricultural and Food Chemistry* 57, no. 12 (2009): 5480–5.

Orsega-Smith, Elizabeth et al. "The Interaction of Stress and Park Use on Psycho-Physiological Health in Older Adults." *Journal of Leisure Research* 36, no. 2 (2004): 232–56. https://doi.org/10.1080/00222216.2004.11950021.

Pallasmaa, Juhani. *The Eyes of the Skin: Architecture and the Senses*. Chichester: Wiley, 2019.

Park, Bum-Jin et al. "Physiological Effects of Forest Recreation in a Young Conifer Forest in Hinokage Town, Japan." *Silva Fennica* 43, no. 2 (2009). https://doi.org/10.14214/sf.213.

Preston, Julieanna. *Interior Atmospheres*. Chichester: Wiley, 2008.

Ray, Julie. "Americans' Stress, Worry and Anger Intensified in 2018," *Gallup*, May 4, 2021. Accessed May 5, 2021. https://news.gallup.com/poll/249098/americans-stress-worry-anger-intensified-2018.aspx.

Schafer, Raymond M. *The Soundscape Our Sonic Environment and the Tuning of the World*. Rochester: Destiny Books, 1993.

Shuang, Han. "Meditation Hall/HIL Architects," *ArchDaily*, February 28, 2019. Accessed May 7, 2021. https://www.archdaily.com/912262/meditation-hall-hil-architects.

Souza, Eduardo. "Peter Zumthor's Therme Vals Through the Lens of Fernando Guerra," *ArchDaily*, October 30, 2016. Accessed May 10, 2021. https://www.archdaily.com/798360/peter-zumthors-therme-vals-through-the-lens-of-fernando-guerra.

Thomas, Gary. *Sacred Pathways: Nine Ways to Connect with God*. Grand Rapids: Zondervan, 2021.

Ulrich, Roger S. et al. "Stress Recovery During Exposure to Natural and Urban Environments." *Journal of Environmental Psychology* 11, no. 3 (1991): 201–30. https://doi.org/10.1016/s0272-4944(05)80184-7.

Zumthor, Peter. *Atmospheres: Architectural Environments, Surrounding Objects*. Basel: Birkhäuser Verlag, 2018.

5 Touring Spaceship Earth

Lisa Claypool

Introduction

In the classic *Operating Manual for Spaceship Earth*, R. Buckminster Fuller observes that "in our schools today" (i.e. 1970, when the book was first published), "we start off the education of our children [in geography] by giving them planes and lines that go on, incomprehendingly 'forever' towards a meaningless infinity."[1] Fuller was writing of a sense of expansiveness structuring the ways in which the planet was (and fifty years later, still is) envisioned in North American public schools, as if everything that could possibly be mapped onto those planes and lines—kangaroos, oak trees, glaciers, butterflies—was reducible to generic points in space that also possessed the potential to expand and grow forever, beyond the limits of sight. Fuller's call for differently envisioning the realities of a planet on the brink of environmental disaster is more urgent than ever today, though many of his own corporate-imperialist design solutions strangely embraced the same kind of expansive geopolitical vision he was critiquing. Yet his point about the place of education in shaping a specialist vision towards Spaceship Earth is well taken.

This chapter proposes "touring" as a series of situational frames through which we become attuned to whatever will get us through; to whatever will aid us in synergetically realizing Fuller's connected world—not from the perspective of a specialist peering at it from the outside, but from within. Specifically, this project takes up a second dimension of the geopolitical mapping of the world in North American schools: the binary of the West/non-West. By questioning the binary through new learning situations that emerged during the pandemic, this project aims to renew a sustainable vision of Spaceship Earth. In short, the aim of the project is to engage with design cultures across the planet for the sake of the engagement itself.

DOI: 10.4324/9781003322726-6

Touring Spaceship Earth 103

What follows is a personal account of my own pedagogical experiments as a professor of design history introducing undergraduate students to sustainable design at the University of Alberta during the years of the COVID lockdown. These experiments were just that: fluid, open-ended, unpredictable. They were not mathematical in their calculus and not controlled in any way. In order to speak to the situated nature of the project, my voice in the following deliberately moves back and forth between the global "we" adopted by Fuller and the personal voice speaking to my own labour in the remote classroom. If the tone becomes polemical at points, it is only because the stakes are so high.

The Urban Generation

We begin not with an exploration of the syllabus to that introductory course, though, but with a painting by a student who has just earned his MFA degree at the university where I teach (Figure 5.1). In it, a skull peers out dimly from behind an astronaut's helmet. Its teeth slide away from an open jaw. Below, vertebrae drop in a string of circles. A skeletal arm reaches up, bone transforming into scaley pipe, and hand into flame or flower. The astronaut-skeleton looks towards unfolding chaos, a swirling constellation of duck heads, bendy airplanes, a syringe (or is it a missile?), monsters that appear to be half-amphibian and half-human, smokestacks, bones, and more skeletons.

Figure 5.1 Jingyu Zhang. Big Thousand World (Daqian shijie 大千世界). 2021. Unmounted handscroll, xuan paper and ink; 40.6 × 482.6 cm. Courtesy of the artist. Photograph by author.

104 Lisa Claypool

The colours of ink rendering this picture—a long unmounted handscroll—do not go far in clarifying the galaxy of things in it. Wet blobs of black ink rest on top of silvery dry brushstrokes. Thin ink washes give some dimension to the ground, but the bare paper also shines through. "Flying white" lines (where the raw paper can be glimpsed beneath the inky mark of the brush) sit next to clusters of darkly scribbled forms.

If this is spaceship earth, something has gone terribly wrong.

In the *Operating Manual for Spaceship Earth*, Fuller muses about the perfect design of our planetary spaceship, and the ominous direction in which it is headed. "Up to now," he writes, "we have been mis-suing, abusing, and polluting this extraordinary chemical energy-interchanging system for successfully regenerating all life aboard our planetary spaceship."[2] How to address our lack of synergy with each other and with the planet? Fuller outlines a systems approach (echoed in the title of the painting, *Big Thousand World* [*Daqian shijie* 大千世界]), a phrase from a Buddhist sutra which less literally translated means "major world system"). He advocates that we think about spaceship earth as if we were city planners "allowed to look at *all* of Philadelphia, and not just peek through a hole at one house or through one door at tone room in that house." He adds, "I think it's appropriate that we assume the role of planners and begin to do the largest scale comprehensive thinking of which we are capable."[3]

But we didn't listen to Fuller. So now, in the twenty-first century, and from the point of view of an artist who is part of the urban generation that inherited the problems from *not* thinking like city planners, Zhang Jingyu's painting pushes us to confront the consequences: a spaceship earth that has become unintelligible to us because of consumption, addiction, industrial pollution, and more. Flying from the beginning of the handscroll to the end changes nothing. There is no place to go in the picture where things make sense. The identity of the skeletons—who they are, what their relation is to each other and to the frog-eyed monsters—is opaque. History, too, is lost to this scrolling non-place of transit and the morass of unidentifiable things and figures pictured in it.

Still, there is a (grim) playfulness to the picture. A sense of humour limning a merry-go-round of skeletal horses, for instance, goes some way in relieving the darkness that the artist shows us, the predicament of the urban generation.

It is precisely this generation who is showing up regularly to the university's introductory course to the History of Art, Design, and Visual Culture (HADVC). They come from small towns and megalopolises around the planet. Nonetheless, despite their sensitivity to their own predicament and its global scale, their expectations for the course are driven by long-lived canons and modes of studying art and design that are centred on the work of white Western Europe and North America. Take, for instance, a comment in the course evaluation of a colleague who taught the course a few terms back: "Asian art has no place in an introductory HADVC course." There is a gap between student appreciation of the synergy of (the dying) spaceship earth as it is represented in the MFA student's *Big Thousand World* painting and the normative geopolitics (literally, the politics of the Earth) that structure canon-approved perspectives on the visual world.

Closing Gaps

What is to be done? In the midst of the pandemic, I had an opportunity to redress this peculiar form of blindness. In the late summer months of 2020, I collaborated with a colleague to redevelop the course. The syllabus is a common one that is to be taught by all of the faculty. It is divided into four sections: essential skills, art history, design issues, and visual culture. Each of my colleagues produced two short teaching videos on topics of their choice that are featured throughout the term along with the recorded lectures by the professor offering the course. It is not a content-driven course, though. We put work by artists and designers from around the globe into the syllabus as a way to learn skills of seeing and to speak fluently about critical issues.

For example, to introduce the language and questions surrounding green architecture, I taught a unit on a project by the "designoloper" and former Dean of the University of Southern California School of Architecture Ma Qingyun and his studio MADA s.p.a.m. in Shenzhen, China. I took the students through the basics about the project, beginning with the question: what is a designoloper? Ma coined this word to talk about situating his architectural projects within the urban and natural surround. A designoloper in his words is an architect who does not design buildings to stand alone as monuments like the Chrysler Building in New York City or the CN Tower in Toronto. A designoloper instead thinks about each building within and in relation to its expanded environment.

Shenzhen is a distant 15-hour flight from the city of Edmonton, where the University of Alberta is located. It is compressed into 2050 square kilometres just north of Hong Kong. I first visited Shenzhen in 1986 when I was a college student and found it to be a relatively unpopulated and muddy place. Barely 73,000 people lived there. Now it is a city with a population of 13.48 million.[4] Parallel to the fact that it is a young city, the average age of city residents is 28 years old, and close to 40% of the people who live in the city are in their 20s. It is a city that buzzes with energy and creativity.

Ma Qingyun asks if this miracle of urban development is turning into misery as nature surrenders to human settlement. His response to his own question took the form of the design project he proposed to a university that was to be located north of the city centre. Ma called the proposed school campus a "new intelligent urban nature settlement."[5]

When school campuses have been designed in the past, they often were planned on a grid, as they are at my university. The natural landscape is cleared away and buildings are constructed along roads that run up and down through it. Ma rejects this thinking about design. Instead of considering the natural space merely to be cleared away so that buildings can be built, he reinterprets building design from a more holistic perspective of sustainable design, which is aimed at designing buildings that harmonize with their surrounding environment and ensure the habitants' health and living environment are impacted in a positive way.

In the rest of the lecture, I focused with some specificity on design elements like the flexible tower allocation, ecological land-use planning, and Ma's attention to the intersection of site, technology, climate and other natural forces, building materials, and so on. He has observed, for example, that "New technologies are all in resistance to natural impact. If there is a wind, there is a tendency to use silicone to resist it. When there is wind load, there is a tendency to resist it, rather than thinking, let's go with the wind a bit, and thereby waste less material, and so on. This leads to—and is based on—a total separation between the constructed world and the organic world."[6]

When I talked about the human dimension of sustainable design, the cultural dimensions of the project also came into view. This aspect of sustainability, in other words, provided me with an opportunity to index theory and practice to ways of seeing that were both global in scope and cultural. For example, I discussed a sketch about allocation of interior space that Ma made on a paper napkin as he was eating steamed dumplings or shao mai for lunch, which he calls the "shao mai strategy" of supporting human activity in a culturally sustainable way. What I think he means by that is that the interior space has its own juicy points of delicious activity, like an art gallery and a hotel for visitors to campus. In one model, you can see how the bridges inside connect different floors and people together. The central open area is a space that opens into the sky and functions as a place for gatherings.

In sum, the investigation into this project brought the relevance of green building in a university context to the attention of the students and, equally, the relevance of design practices through the eyes of a Chinese architect who works around the globe. The skill it was intended to foster in this case had to do with developing an understanding of some of the basic concepts of sustainable architectural design. Sustainable technology and design principles, however, are coupled to local and often to cultural needs. In that sense, this teaching case study literally gave students another way to see spaceship earth.

The West/Non-West

And yet I discovered only weeks after drafting the common syllabus that a key session dedicated to teaching students about perspective was reworked by the professor then teaching the course. Pictures like *Big Thousand World* that might have encouraged students to ponder one-point perspective in oil paintings (and the power relationships they establish that are discussed by John Berger in *Ways of Seeing*, a book assigned in the course) were marked as "optional," for instance, with a note to the effect of "if you want to learn more, I encourage you to take upper-level courses with the two Asianists in the faculty." When questioned, the professor responded that she could not teach everything and therefore was focusing on the West.

It was at this point that I realized that it wasn't simply the weight of the canon that was the problem. The "West," and further, the lurking binary of the West/non-West behind it, was structuring thinking behind the course delivery and was equally troubling. Indeed, this was captured in the class reading assignments. Outside of the constant reference to "Western painting" or "Western visual culture," at least one of the texts that had always been taught in the course relies directly on the binary. Dana Arnold reflects in her popular Oxford University Press textbook *Art History: A Very Short Introduction* (republished in a second edition in 2020) that "In the case of non-Western art, everyday objects, sometimes referred to as material culture, are the best evidence we have for the artistic output of a given society."[7]

This should give pause. One of the many questions it raises is: where is the "non-West?" Where does "the West" end and the rest of the world begin? To get at an answer to that question, we first would have to define "the West." It is a term that came into use during the colonial enterprises of white European courts during the seventeenth and eighteenth centuries. The West (capital W) is not the same as a geographic orientation (lower case w). The West is a subject position. It is a position of authority. And it is a strangely and deliberately blinded one, for not only does it insist on a certain defining power over the "non-," but it also fails to recognize the power of the "non-" in shaping the cultural formations of the "West." We might instead think of the complexities of culture produced, for instance, through "the multicultural empire, *mestizaje*, intercultural encounters, liberal revolutions."[8]

These binaries are so much part of our current geopolitics that they appear in everyday language across the globe. Such language colours sensitive political conversations about race-based discrimination, environmental justice, and more.[9] For instance, a recent wonderful book about twentieth-century Chinese feminism published in the States finds critical importance in "engaging contemporary feminist theoretical discourse in broader terms than the well-known debates over the theoretical priorities of gender, sex, sexuality, sexual difference, identity politics, or intersectionality that have dominated contemporary Euro-American feminist discussion over the past few decades." Yet the book also takes as its raison de être "rescuing the voice of non-Western feminists."[10] This, in spite of sensitivity to Gayatri Spivak's critique of "the ironclad opposition of West and East," is also referenced in the book's introduction.[11] And in another recent publication on made-in-China feminism, the abstract ends with the thought that the "analysis contributes to the ongoing conversation on imagining a feminist politics in non-Western societies that disrupts the political, economic, and cultural orders all at once."[12]

On the other hand, these scholars might be onto something. Is it possible to consider the "non-" as a position of agency and resistance? Perhaps. Culture critic and curator Okwui Enwezor talks about the possibilities of such a position in precisely those terms: "Post-Westernism has to do with the skepticism in the non-Western world toward the essential wisdom that is the monopoly of the West. And so, in order to think about the future, to project forward, we need different lenses—it cannot be a singular lens."[13]

And it is important to acknowledge that this language is grounded in a long history of abuses of power and claims for those monopolies of wisdom. Yet the conundrum is that today, in a different world, a "post-Western" world, with R. Buckminster Fuller's forecasts about "the direction in which all humanity is trending"[14] ringing in our ears, we still are committed to the dark geopolitics embedded in this binary. In twenty-first-century China, for example, from the perspective of one of the designated "nons," the binary still is normative. It is usually articulated as "China/the West." It's strange because China has had many Wests, and they often were distinguished in the historical record. In the nineteenth century, for example, France was not England was not Holland. It was only after the National Essence Movement around the 1910s that the language became explicitly political, the "West" was confirmed to be a power worth emulating, and "China" emerged through a newly scripted 5000-year Han-centric history. Today the "West" denotes white North American and Western European cultures outside of the boundaries of China. It may denote more. It's hard to say. It is as much about an oppositional "us" and "them" as it is an acknowledgement of those long-lived structures of power. It is imbued with a whiff of a kind of performed self-Orientalization—a means of writing a line under re-essentialized cultural difference (think of the spectacular 2008 Beijing Olympics Opening Ceremony), and in the most positive way of spinning it, it strengthens national autonomy.[15]

I often tell my students that any sentence that begins with the words "the Chinese people think" or "the Canadians believe" is one that you cannot finish without being wrong. How much more true is that for the West and the non-West?

The bind of course is that current academic discourse goes in the direction of accepting the language of "Western" design or art *as if that were the politically correct thing to do* rather than stopping to ask what it is that we mean when we talk about people and cultures using this blanketing language (and especially the language of the "non-"). To be sure, there are shifts to speaking of "Euro-America" instead of the "West." Or as Lorraine Justice puts it in a book about China's design revolutions, we might consider "Western" and "Eastern" cultures. She writes, for example, that "products produced for both Eastern and Western cultures should be analyzed in both cultural contexts."[16] However, that second *both* reveals the thinking behind the language: there are two world cultures, and if China is the benchmark for the "East," those "Eastern and Western cultures" as she portrays them turn out to be opposites and inversions in processes of creativity and design. So the new and newly employed terms collapse many cultures into one, sometimes replicate very precisely the historical and colonial thinking about the West/non-West, and highlight a lack of awareness and attunement to the ways (what Fuller might call a systems approach) that visual culture, art, and design are made up as we go along in culturally complex spaces where the "other" (whether that is the "non-" or not) is very much present.

But there is even more to this problem of the "West" and its "nons" within the academy. Design historian Arindam Dutta makes precisely this point in his brilliant book about the British Department of Science and Art's (DSA) design education, and museological and exhibition practices during the late nineteenth century in the "non-West," and specifically in Britain's prime colony, India. *Design*, as Dutta defines it, is prosaic (such as the pattern or motif on your clothes) *and* a "comprehensive, rationalizing, future-oriented intention" that embodies a particular vision of industrialist capitalism.[17] Rather than framing "Western" knowledge interpolated in design thinking and feeling as if it makes uni-dimensional and essentialized the "non-Western subject," or as if it is a prison house of design ideology, he writes of the ways that the DSA's regulated aesthetics of design possessed fungibility. The embrace of wonder, and the possibility for misreadings and failures of understanding even within the scientific rationality informing design, allowed the DSA to accommodate the "cognitive failures" of the subaltern. This seems threatening for its totalizing power. And yet it also underlined the fact that other meanings and interpretations of those systems from within and through different local systems were possible and realized, though not actually recognized for what they were by the DSA. One effect of continuing today to perceive design in the DSA's universal terms as civilization, Dutta observes, and relevant for this chapter on design history pedagogy, is that,

> With the ongoing shifts of transnational investment and the changed clientele of American universities, curricula have borne an increased emphasis on "non-Western" or global content. Produced as this demand is by the features of contemporary globalization, with its marked bias against the (welfare) state, studies and curricula pertaining to "non-Western" peoples have tended to ignore the infrastructural supports of the aesthetic.[18]

The educational system clearly is one of those infrastructural supports. What Dutta's book calls for, in effect, is attunement to what is not seen when the "universal" aesthetics of "the West" give the eye a lens that blinds it to alterity and to the need for radical histories of "non-Western" aesthetic and design practices. It asks for attention, not to the inclusion of "non-Western" art and design within "Western" structures of an aesthetic, but attention to the structure (and infrastructure) itself. To resite the formation and pedagogy of design histories not only is a way of questioning the geopolitics of the language of the West and its nons but also is a way of testing the power and fungibility of the educational situation itself.

Seeking Synergy

Teaching the course online during the 2021 winter and fall, academic terms provided me with an unexpected opportunity to *practice* art, design, and visual culture history as a way of vascularly connecting student awareness of Spaceship Earth and its shared crises back to awareness of the ethics of seeing the visual world. Which is to say, rather than simply providing students with knowledge of basic skills and language that they would need to practice art and design history, and in my lectures, showing them how to do so, or relying on written assignments to get them to start finding the relevance of these lessons, I created a special space for students to put knowledge into practice. This practice made the inclusion of design from across the globe not simply an added dimension to the course but also began to disrupt the usual educational infrastructure itself.

At each week's end, I took students on optional virtual field trips to museums and sites. We visited São Paulo, Mexico City, Tokyo, Paris, Budapest, Vancouver, Stonehenge in northern England, London, Toronto, Seoul, and Beijing.[19] I chose the museums in part because of their virtual presence. Could we "walk" into the gallery space? Would we have to contend with extensive curatorial prose telling us how to see and interpret the work? How close could we get to it? If the work was a video installation, would we be able to watch the video online? Would the work of art or design and display, in sum, lend itself to being encountered in a virtual space?

I brought along a graduate teaching assistant to help launch an open conversation (and to monitor the chat function as well). Our stated goal was to practice a particular skill (for example, visual analysis, iconographic analysis) or to ask a particular question (what is design?). At each viewing, we entered the museum space, virtually strolled the galleries, and talked at length about two to three objects. I then gave students five minutes to explore, email screenshots of things they found absorbing to me, and we ended the session with a discussion of one of those.

One value to this expansive itinerary, and a critical criterion to my thinking about venues to visit in this project, was that we were able to get into spaces where artworks and works of design are not displayed only to create important conversations around issues what Eve Tuck defines as "damage-centered" narratives[20] such as racism and gender. As the painter Kay WalkingStick observes, there are political stakes to this project. "Critical questions that would be raised in other venues simply are not considered in ethnic- or gender-specific exhibitions.

Not to receive serious critical review is a kind of disempowerment."[21] Instead, we visited exhibitions with more mainstream themes that included so-called "non-" artists and designers. An example of an exhibition with a mainstream theme would be "Looking for Family" at the National Museum of Modern and Contemporary Art in Seoul. The curatorial project was to expand the word *family* "beyond its traditional definition, where it is primarily used to emphasize biological or/and marital relationships, and in doing so deal … with the importance of addressing a problem from diverse perspectives based on the different experiences and values of individuals."[22] In addition, solo exhibitions like "Who's Afraid of Teresinha Soares?" at the MASP, São Paulo, as well as the galleries devoted to Frida Kahlo in the Museo Dolores Olmedo, Mexico City, allowed artworks by individual artists to be encountered on their own terms.

At the beginning of the unit on design, we travelled to the Museum of Applied Arts in Budapest. That week we had read a wonderful essay by Louise Schouwenberg.[23] She writes about a cabinet that existed half-invisibly at the interstices of family aspirations to have the biggest, most beautiful, and most useful cabinet, the crushing disappointment after it was finally purchased, constructed, and moved into the home at its monster-size presence there and, subsequently, its place within the spaces of memory, though the cabinet was eventually reduced to smaller pieces and in the end left on the garbage heap. The meaning of the cabinet "resided not solely in its function, in its problem-solving capacity—we were indeed able to store an abundance of items in it—but apparently we had anticipated more satisfaction, greater happiness even, and certainly more prolonged pride at the display of prestige and wealth it represented (any pride at our good taste had evaporated the minute the thing arrived at our house)."[24] She quotes Pierre Bourdieu: "taste classifies, and it classifies the beholder."[25] She finishes the essay by mapping taste against consumerism, concluding "what was designed yesterday and is produced today has consequences for tomorrow. Terms such as 'defuturing' and 'cradle-to-cradle' have been fashionable for some time in relation to the importance of an awareness of the consequences of unbridled production and consumption."[26]

Prompted by Shouwenberg's discussion of the emotional, social, and ethical complexities to beholding and owning a piece of furniture, at the museum, we focused on domestic objects. For example, we spent some time with a glass vase by the French designer Émile Gallé (1846–1904) (Figure 5.2). The vase is solid and squat. Its weight and sense of immovability are enhanced by a heavy, flared foot and

Touring Spaceship Earth 113

Figure 5.2 Émile Gallé. Vase with insect. Layered glass, h: 16 cm, maximum w: 15 cm. Courtesy of the Museum of Applied Arts, Budapest.

lip, and a bulging midsection. Iridescent silver-grey, ultramarine blue, and a penumbra of luminous black, something like spilled sumi ink, trail over the surface. A cricket and other insect forms are appliqued to the centre of its thick neck. Zoom magnification allowed us to move in close and see the dense opacity of the glass cricket and the bony texture of its body, forked legs, and curving antennae. The detail is practically millimetric. Yet the curve of the vase surface imparted a dimensionality to the insect that contradicted its specimen-like flatness. The look of the design thus could be located in a resonate space between science and art, grounded by the vase's heavy thingness—its facticity—cast against the effervescent clouds of colours. The vase in fact was designed right around the time that the Japanese forester, geologist, and artist Takashima Hokkai 高島北海 (1850–1931) was sojourning in Nancy, France, and working with Gallé. They shared an interest in insects. The design is informed not so much by an imaginary sense of the exotic (hinted at by that inky black, perhaps) as it is by real cultural exchange. The aliveness of the insect and of the vase as a domestic object in Schouwenberg's terms grew near the longer we engaged with its cultural embodiments.

And we did *engage*. Coming together to collectively explore inspired a sense of virtual nearness with each other as well as the object focus of our attention, rather than estrangement. It turned out to be a way to pool knowledge (one of the teaching assistants is Brazilian; there were students present who have deep personal connections to Mexico City, Paris, and Tokyo; I have lived and studied in the Tokyo area and knew the museum there as well as the one in Seoul; all of the students were on the webs, anyway, and able to easily use search engines to answer specific questions). It gave the students confidence to go beyond conventional assessments based on period style, form, dates, and times, and instead to dwell with the vase for an extended moment, long enough to see and remark on the texture of the glass, the sparkle of light on the dark surface, the push and pull between the heaviness of the glass form against its delicate ornamentation. We were able to feel the presence of the physically absent vase online through the way it evoked thought and emotion. We *oriented* to the vase in a way that was almost tangible because of the way it occupied our collective perception.

Conclusion

"One of the things I do enjoy about the field trips is that the class can actually gather and discuss art and ideas together," a student wrote, "rather than slog through readings and then have no meaningful way to follow up those readings other than assignments." But how to gauge the effectiveness of this pedagogical adventure? What did the students take away from our gatherings and discussions of art, design, and ideas?

A significant point of value in this project is that it built students' confidence in their own ability to say what they see. Partly this had to do with speaking from the safety of their own home. "I really like how we're at home," a student noted, "but we can go around the world and learn the arts." Partly it had to do with learning from other students. "Somebody always notices something in a different way than I do, and it really broadens how I look at art. I also just enjoy being exposed to more works of art." Mostly, it was in that moment of collaborating, and pooling thoughts and impressions, that the fear of saying something wrong that typically prevents students from saying anything (especially within new cultural contexts) began to dissipate. "The field trips are enhancing my learning experience in the course. I like that we get to interact the with artwork ourselves and can throw out ideas in a setting where there are no grades or an expectation to be perfect, it's all about learning."

The objects and pictures students wrote about or videographed in the assignments go some way in demonstrating attunement to cultural difference without dismissal, fear, or blindness to it (recall the student who believed that Asian art had no place in an introductory HADVC course). These assignments were not interpretive in nature, but exploratory. They did not ask for research. For example, in the design unit, students were asked to analyse a work of design and at the end raise a question that emerged from that deep visual engagement—to let the work of design suggest the question, and to think about why they were asking that particular question and not another. They could choose the focal design for the assignment. Students elected to write about the Bahrain World Trade Center, the Eden Project in Cornwall, a waste to energy recycling plant in Copenhagen, a Fujian Earth Building in China, the Théâtre de verdure at the Ville de Montréal, Choi+Shine Architects' Land of Giants project for Iceland, and Nagoya Castle in Japan. And they also wrote about things designed in other places that ended up in their homes, like Polish Bolesławiec pottery, a Ukrainian vinok, the San Francisco zine *Fat Girl*, and a Japanese sticky memo pad. The simple fact that they were moving around the planet is encouraging. Their willingness to *practice* seeing and saying what they see with open curiosity and awareness of a kind of subject-subject relationship between beholder and design also is encouraging.

But I am not sanguine. When the students lapse back into using the geopolitical language of the West in future (as it is such a normalized part of academic and everyday discourse, it's hard to see that they won't), my hope nonetheless is that the object lessons of the course will prove to be a productive failure: that in the back of their minds, a voice will be questioning, perhaps the voice of Buckminster Fuller, about what might be gained if only we're willing to risk a change in our perspective on the way we envision and inhabit Spaceship Earth.

Notes

1 Fuller, *Operating Manual for Spaceship Earth* (New York: Pocket Books, 1970), 20.
2 Fuller, *Operating Manual for Spaceship Earth*, 46–47.
3 Fuller, *Operating Manual for Spaceship Earth*, 52–53.
4 Shenzhen Government Online/深圳政府在线 (May 28, 2021 statistics). Doi: http://www.sz.gov.cn/en_szgov/aboutsz/profile/content/post_1357629.html.

5 Lecture delivered at the Reed College campus in conjunction with the V&A's *China Design Now* exhibition at the Portland Art Museum during October, 2009.
6 Stephen Wright, "A City without Leftovers: A Conversation with Ma Qingyun," in *Shanghai Kaleidoscope,* ed. Christopher Phillips (Toronto: ICC at the ROM, 2008), 37.
7 Dana Arnold, *Art History: A Very Short Introduction,* 2nd ed. (Oxford: Oxford University Press, 2020), 9.
8 Marta Araújo and Silvia R. Maeso, eds., *Eurocentrism, Racism and Knowledge: Debates on History and Power in Europe and the Americas* (Basingstoke: Palgrave Macmillan, 2015), 3.
9 Relevant to our discussion of Spaceship Earth, the book *Arts of Living on a Damaged Planet* begins with an introduction to our haunted landscapes in which the writers aver that "As anthropologists, we imagine our talk of ghosts in kinship with community around the world, Western and non-Western, who offer nonsecular descriptions of the landscape and its hauntings." The assertion of a strangely geopoliticized world community is followed by a contradictory thought: "The book is not about cosmologies [which I take to be ideologically-freighted visions of how the world is], but rather about on-the-ground observations, and from varied historical diffractions and points of view." See Anna Tsing, Heather Swanson, Elaine Gan, and Nils Bubandt, "Introduction: Haunted Landscapes of the Anthropocene," in *Arts of Living on a Damaged Planet* (Minneapolis: University of Minnesota Press, 2017), 2–3.
10 Rebecca Karl, Lydia Liu, Dorothy Ko, "Introduction: Toward a Transnational Feminist Theory" in *The Birth of Chinese Feminism: Essential Texts in Transnational Theory*, eds. Karl, Liu, Ko (New York: Columbia University Press, 2013), 4.
11 Karl, et al., "Introduction," 7.
12 Angela Xiao Wu and Yige Dong, "What is made-in-China feminism(s)? Gender discontent and class friction in post-Socialist China," *Critical Asian Studies* 51, no. 4 (2019): 471.
13 "Okwui Enwezor talks with Michelle Kuo about the Upcoming 56th Venice Biennale," *Artform* (May 2015). Doi: https://www.artforum.com/print/201505/okwui-enwezor-talks-with-michelle-kuo-about-the-upcoming-56th-venice-biennale-51556
14 Fuller, *Operating Manual for Spaceship Earth,* 10.
15 See Arif Dirlik, "Chinese History and the Question of Orientalism," *History and Theory* 35, no. 4 (December 1996): 96–118.
16 Lorraine Justice, *China's Design Revolution* (Cambridge, MA: MIT Press, 2012), 4.
17 Arindam Dutta, *The Bureaucracy of Beauty: Design in the Age of its Social Reproducibility* (New York: Routledge, 2007), 5.
18 Dutta, *Bureaucracy,* 36.
19 "Who's Afraid of Teresinha Soares?" at the MASP, São Paulo; galleries devoted to Frida Kahlo in the Museo Dolores Olmedo, Mexico City; the National Museum of Art, Tokyo; Musée d'Orsay, Paris; Museum of Applied Arts, Budapest; The Centre for Interactive Research on Sustainability, UBC, Vancouver; the British Museum, London; Nathan

Eugene Carson, "Cut from the Same Cloth," The Power Plant, Toronto; "Looking for Another Family," National Museum of Modern and Contemporary Art, Seoul; "Experimental Art at the 21st National Art Exhibition" (Song Dong, Lu Zhigang, Jiang Xinyu), Today Art Museum, Beijing.
20 Eve Tuck, "Suspending Damage: A Letter to Communities," *Harvard Educational Review* 79, no. 3 (Fall 2009): 409.
21 Kay WalkingStick, "Native American Art in the Postmodern Era," *Art Journal* 51, no. 3 (1992): 15.
22 Doi: https://artsandculture.google.com/exhibit/looking-for-another-family/vgLC7490hh3wKA.
23 Louise Schouwenberg, "A Cabinet," in *BEYOND the NEW on the Agency of THINGS*, eds. Schouwenberg and Hella Jongerius (London: Koenig Books, 2018), 24–37.
24 Schouwenberg, "A Cabinet," 25.
25 Schouwenberg, "A Cabinet," 28.
26 Schouwenberg, "A Cabinet," 33.

Bibliography

Araújo, Marta and Maeso, Silvia R., eds. *Eurocentrism, Racism and Knowledge: Debates on History and Power in Europe and the Americas.* Basingstoke: Palgrave Macmillan, 2015.

Arnold, Dana. *Art History: A Very Short Introduction.* 2nd ed. Oxford: Oxford University Press, 2020.

Berger, John. *Ways of Seeing.* London: BBC, 1972.

Bourdieu, Pierre. *Distinction: A Social Critique of the Judgement of Taste.* Tr. Richard Nice. Cambridge, MA: Harvard University Press, 1984.

Çapan, Zeynep Gülşah. "Eurocentrism and the Construction of the 'Non-West.'" *E-International Relations* (June 19, 2018), https://www.e-ir.info/2018/06/19/eurocentrism-and-the-construction-of-the-non-west/

Dirlik, Arif. "Chinese History and the Question of Orientalism." *History and Theory* 35, no. 4 (December 1996): 96–118.

Dutta, Arindam. *The Bureaucracy of Beauty: Design in the Age of its Social Reproducibility.* New York: Routledge, 2007.

"Okwui Enwezor talks with Michelle Kuo about the Upcoming 56th Venice Biennale." 2015. *Artform* (May). Doi: https://www.artforum.com/print/201505/okwui-enwezor-talks-with-michelle-kuo-about-the-upcoming-56th-venice-biennale-51556

Fuller, Buckminster R. *Operating Manual for Spaceship Earth.* Pocket Book ed. New York: Pocket Books, 1970.

Hall, Stuart. "The West and the Rest: Discourse and Power [1992]." In *Essential Essays, Vol. 2: Identity and Diaspora.* Ed. David Morely, 141–84. Durham: Duke University Press, 2019.

Jānī, Vibhāvarī. *Diversity in Design: Perspectives from the Non-Western World.* London: Bloomsbury, 2011.

Justice, Lorraine. *China's Design Revolution*. Cambridge, Mass: MIT Press, 2012.
Karl, Rebecca, Lydia Liu, Dorothy Ko. "Introduction: Toward a Transnational Feminist Theory." In *The Birth of Chinese Feminism: Essential Texts in Transnational Theory*. Eds. Lydia H. Liu, Rebecca E. Karl, and Dorothy Ko, 1–26. New York: Columbia University Press, 2013.
McNamara, Andrew. "Review: Critical Reckonings: Global Art and Art History after the West and Eurocentrism." *Art Journal* 74, no. 3 (Fall 2015): 67–9.
Mosquera, Gerardo. "The Marco Polo Syndrome: Some Problems around Art and Eurocentrism." In *Theory in Contemporary Art Since 1985*. Eds. Zoya Kocur and Simon Leong, 314–8. Malden, MA: Blackwell, 2005.
Oguibe, Olu. "In the 'Heart of Darkness.'" In *Theory in Contemporary Art Since 1985*. Eds. Zoya Kocur and Simon Leong, 324–7. Malden, MA: Blackwell, 2005.
Said, Edward. *Orientalism*. New York: Penguin Books, 1978.
Schouwenberg, Louise. "A Cabinet." In *BEYOND the NEW on the Agency of THINGS*. Eds. Schouwenberg and Hella Jongerius, 24–37. London: Koenig Books, 2018.
Tsing, Anna, Heather Swanson, Elaine Gan, and Nils Bubandt. "Introduction: Haunted Landscapes of the Anthropocene." In *Arts of Living on a Damaged Planet*. Eds. Tsing, Swanson, Gan, Bubandt, 1–14. Minneapolis, MN: University of Minnesota Press, 2017.
Tuck, Eve. "Suspending Damage: A Letter to Communities." *Harvard Educational Review* 79, no. 3 (Fall 2009): 409–28.
WalkingStick, Kay. "Native American Art in the Postmodern Era." *Art Journal* 51, no. 3 (1992): 15–7.
Wright, Stephen. "A City without Leftovers: A Conversation with Ma Qingyun." In *Shanghai Kaleidoscope*. Ed. Christopher Phillips, 30–9. Toronto: ICC at the ROM, 2008.
Wu, Angela X., Yige Dong. "What is made-in-China feminism(s)? Gender discontent and class friction in post-Socialist China." *Critical Asian Studies* 51, no. 4 (2019): 471–92.

Conclusion

Sean Burns and Matthew Wilson

As a collection of essays, this study challenges disciplinary connotations of site and its distinctive qualities. It poses a series of pedagogical questions for how sites might be diversely interpreted and introduced to design students. This book examines notions of introducing sensory phenomena about site while in remote locations. It explores unorthodox notions of site as the impetus to creativity, and it delves into managing and maintaining the finite qualities of site. Moreover, this book discusses activating site as a participant throughout the design process. It offers approaches to scholarship of teaching and learning with respect to diverse readings of site within design education. The aim herein is to share alternative notions of site and innovative and progressive design studio pedagogy.

Chelsea Limbird introduces iterations of a project that embraced the concept of memory and atmosphere through multiple lenses. Questioning the limits of our senses, Limbird asks students to create atmospheres by which they imagined new situational sites based on personal recollections. The evolution of the students' work probes the boundaries of site and gives new meaning to the term atmosphere, which embraces both the product and process of the work from her students. The memory is mined as a form of research that aids in the creation of atmospheres that represent a vision for new spatial experiences in the future. This approach allows for innovative forms of creating conceptual art that is embedded with personal thoughts, feelings, and experiences. In this sense, students draw on the virtual world of the mind as the data and lore of the artefact.

Emily Bereskin and Natacha Quintero González apply multi-scalar strategies for critical cartography that likewise call on the imagination. Here, they develop thematic teaching strategies of site-led research and design pedagogy that prompt students to link their daily experiences in the home to global networks, varying socio-political contexts, flows, and ecological systems. This process enables students to conceptualize site, space and city as flows, linkages, and in terms of relationality as opposed to strictly material constructions. Students became aware that they did not have access to all the information necessary for their research. When their desktop video documentary projects called for more synthetic or analytic analyses, they felt emboldened to imagine and create their own evidence to fill the gaps in knowledge. This became a way to teach students the value of interpretation, debate, and the use of a variety of different sources and interpretations in the practice of academic writing.

Chapter 3 asks readers to recast site in architectural design pedagogy by examining what constitutes a situational setting. Here, it is argued that preconceived notions of site should not be strictly reduced to that of the ground with defined metes and boundaries. Alternatively, students are urged to construct site as a series of surrogate conditions rooted in literature, social and environmental justice, philosophy, sociology, and material studies. Consequently, designers are persuaded to no longer restrict site to a tract of topography at a specific locale that they might deem subordinate to an architectural object. By reimagining alternative origins of sites, students might expand their purview and appreciation of site, thus promoting it as an active agent throughout the design process. The studies within this chapter reflect upon how site is considered, developed, and substantiated as a generative tangible or imagined entity.

Thereafter, in Chapter 4, Lisa Phillips steps beyond the visual by way of employing phenomenological analysis of the exterior environment to produce richer multisensory interior design solutions. This charge calls on design students to consider more fully the design of the passage between the interior and exterior experiences. It likewise led students to think about their experiential agendas. Here they seek to make connections beyond the strictly visual. They consider how a wide range of stimuli can inform the place-making process to create a deeper immersive and thus memorable space. In this sense, Phillips points to the creation of a context that might serve as the basis for Limbird's students, who seek to draw on localized experiences as the driver of creating new spaces of hope.

In the final chapter, Lisa Claypool explores using a skills-based approach to teach the history of design with an aim to disrupt notions of the 'West' versus the 'other'. Claypool offers a weekly virtual tour to a museum or site across the planet. In this manner, site is presented as a situational event – a tour. No longer restricted by distance, proximity, and ability to travel, the domain of site is broadened.

Conclusion   121

Similar to Bereskin and Quintero González, Claypool introduced videography and writing assignments that encouraged students to explore cultural difference without dismissal, fear, or blindness. This process was not about research. Instead, Claypool encouraged students to reflect on their inherent biases. In this way, they developed a practice of questioning their curiosities. Thus, the idea of site spoke to fostering an equitable subject-subject relationship as opposed to a subject-subjected, subject-object, or colonizer-colonized perspective.

As such, in the postmodern tradition of Jean-François Lyotard, these chapters suggest a new taxonomy for site born from reflection and experimentation. They expand parameters to encourage plurality and diversity in terms of a variety of interpretations of site. They speak of the virtual, the immaterial, the literary, the philosophical, and the imaginative, and thus they de-centre conventional connotations of site within design education. The studies detailed in this book encourage students to formulate a conscientious commitment to values and ethical stances at various levels of the design process. In this sense, the lessons presented within the book's chapters speak to a demand of wanting something more from site as a place of activity and more so as a place for reflection, thinking, and meaning in the creative process.

Taking this forward, we see site as a vessel that contains various meanings and opportunities at the intersection of theory and practice. It is a nexus for critical reflection and mental activity that engrains geometry with cultural significance. By expanding the boundaries of site, designers might appreciate it as a moment of interaction between mind and media. In this way, we seek to foster a sensitivity of craft and a desire to produce creations worth caring for and worth preserving for future generations.

Index

Italicized and **bold** pages refer to figures and tables respectively, and page numbers followed by "n" refer to notes.

absolute architecture 52
absolute material space 52
Adaptation Case Study 20–24
adaptive reuse 20, 22, 24, 26
Adobe Premiere Pro 40
Allen, S. 56
Anderson, J. 68
Arbery, A. 68
architectural design 2, 61, 64, 69, 120; characteristic of 58; process 55; projects 5
architectural design studio 51, 53, 57, 65, 68
architecture: boundary in 3; classical language of 54; creative process in 4; discipline of 30; figurated object of 61; future of 51; teaching and learning in 68; tea plantations of 37; use of 34; *see also* interior architecture
Arnold, D. 107, 109, 110
Art History: A Very Short Introduction (Arnold) 107
atmosphere 82, 119; collections of 13; spatial experiences of 10; time in 19–20
Atmospheres of the Day 13–18
Audacity 40
auditory-visual time-based presentation 14
Augé, M. 54
Augmented Landscapes (Allen) 56
Aureli, P. V. 52

Baudoin, G. S. 2
Baudrillard, J. 54
bean paste painting 15
beet sugar 35
Bereskin, E. 119, 121
Berger, J. 107
Big Thousand World painting *103*, 104, 105, 107
birds, lives and habitats of 25
Black Lives Matter 68
'Bloody Sunday Memorial pavilion' 69, *70*
boundary conditions 56–60
Bourdieu, P. 112
British Department of Science and Art's (DSA) 110
Brooks, R. 68
Burks, D. *63*
Burns, S. 5
Burrows, D. 32

Cache, B. 56
camera phone, use of 38
Canaday, J. *70*
Carrasquilla, K. *66*
Castellón, J. 58
Chaplin, C. 26
China 25, 105, 108, 109, 115
cinema 26–27
Claypool, L. 6, 120, 121
Coleman, N. 63
color 15, 16, 25; graphics of 24; plates 14

Index   123

communication, techniques of 12
Computer Aided Design (CAD) 34, 38
conceptualized spaces 55
Conley, N. *70*
contemporary technology 53, 54
COVID-19 pandemic 11, 30
creative process 2, 4, 69, 121
Crow, J. 67
Cruz, B. *61*

"damage-centered" narratives 111
Daniyam, J. *70*
Darjeeling tea production 35, *37*
Darling, A. 84
death of modernism 62
density study 85, 89, 93
design 1, 3; education and practice 68; exterior 80; interior 79; pedagogy 2; process of 3, 10; tools and methodologies 21
desktop documentaries 38–43
Diderot, D. 64, 65
digital learning 5, 30; *see also* online teaching

Earth 32, 58, 60
ecological systems 29, 120
Edmund Pettus Bridge 69
El-Setouhy, H. 57
Emerging Practices in Architectural Pedagogy (Sanderson and Stone) 2
emotional attachments 16
Empire Quarry 57, *59*
Empire State Building 57
environment: exterior 5; image, color and texture 15; interior 90; urban 18
Enwezor, O. 108
Evans, R. 58
exterior sensory analysis 97
The Eyes of the Skin (Pallasmaa) 84

'Feeding the City' 32
fictitious website *42*
film(s): academic expression in 40; clips 14, 19; editing tools 19; Hollywood 19; techniques of 13
Floyd, G. 68

'follow-the-thing' research 30, 33, 43
food cycle 32–38
food retail 34
food sovereignty movements 34
food systems 32, 35, 38, 40
Frampton, K. 58
'From the Region' 32, 39
Fuller, R. B. 102, 104, 108, 115

Gallé, E. 112, *113*
geographical site 21, 29
geographic information systems (GIS) 31
Gerardot, A. *63*
Glissant, E. 54, 67
González, J. 58
González, N. Q. 119, 121
Google Images 39
green pea paste 15
green watercolor 15
Gregotti, V. 56
Groundscapes (Ilka and Ruby) 2

Hartoonian, G. 54
Harvey, D. 52, 55
Hensel, M. 52
Hil Architects' Meditation Hall 84
Hochgesang, C. *61, 63*
Hokkai, T. 112
Hollywood films 19, 20
Hood, W. 67
'Huis Clos' 65, *66*
Hungry City: How Food Shapes Our Lives (Steel) 33
Hurst, A. *94*
Hu, X. *22*

iMovie 40
industrialization 26
Ingold, T. 61, 62
'Instigating Mass' 65, *66*
interior architecture 14
interior design 80, 83, 88, 91, 98
Interpreting Site: Studies in Perception, Representation, and Design (Baudoin) 2
interstellar cinema 26–27

Jencks, C. 62

landscapes 14, 16, 54, 60, 67; accessible and physical 51; architects 88; cultural, economic and social 24; natural 106; urban 19
layered glass *113*
learning: digital 5; experience in 114; practices of 42; remote 53
Leatherbarrow, D. 3, 53, 55, 60
Lee, K. B. 39
Leibham, J. *66*
Leski, K. 2
Liard, M. *66*
Limbird, C. 4, 119, 120
Lynn, G. 53
Lyotard, J.-F. 61, 62

Magix Video Deluxe 40
making, process of 14–15
mapping methodology 33
Ma Qingyun 106
Marcuse, H. 54
Marian County Court House 69
material space 54; absolute properties of 52, 64
material studies 6, 14, 51, 120
McFarlane, C. 31
McLean, K. 87
Medina, R. *63*
Mei, Y. *23*
'Memorial for the Charleston Church Massacre' 69, *70*
memories, visualizations of 13
mental stress 16
Merleau-Ponty, M. 81
Mitchell, W. 54
modernization 26, 54
"*Modern Times*" (film) 26
Montagu, A. 81
'Museum of American Violence' 68
Museum of Applied Arts 112, *113*
Mutable Sites 24, *25*

National Essence Movement 109
Nolan, J. *66*

online classroom 11
online education: desktop documentaries 38–43; troubles 29

online teaching 29, 30, 43; *see also* online education
Operating Manual for Spaceship Earth (Fuller) 102, 104
Pallasmaa, J. 81, 84
pandemic-engendered sites 64–66
pedagogy 2, 10, 11, 110; of site values 52
Phenomenology of Perception (Merleau-Ponty) 81
Philadelphia 93, 104
Phillips, L. 5, 120
physical sensory boxes 91
physical site 5, 21, 34, 35, 71
political memory 67–70
Po-Mo Church 62, *63*
Porter, N. *70*
post-Fordism 62
post-industrialization 62
postmodern architecture 62
postmodern classicism 62
postmodernism 62
post-Westernism 108
psychological stress 16

QuickTime 40

Race and Ethnic Relations (Anderson) 68
Rajchman, J. 53
Reid, C. *92*
'Remembering the Baltimore Uprising' 69, *70*
remote studio 10, 53
'Room and [bill]Board' 60, *61*
Ruby, A. 2, 53
Ruby, I. 2, 53

Sanderson, L. 2
Sartre, J.-P. 65
Schafer, R. M. 87
Schouwenberg, L. 112, 114
Schumacher, P. 52
screen-based classroom 11
self-created website *42*
self-study 12
Semper, G. 58
sensory experience 14, 17, 18, 20, 21, 88, 93

sensory maps 85, *86*
"Sensory Upgrade, Before/After Collage" 24, *25*
sepia tone photograph 15
Shipp, T. 69
Shi, S. *25*
silent film 19
site(s) 1, 30, 51, 119; Pandemic-engendered, paradigm of 64–66; atmospheric ascent 52–55; communication of 20; documentation in 18; eternal construction 20; material and social production of 31; observation in 18; physical and geographical 21; political and social mediascape 67–70; pre-pandemic reconsiderations of 60–63; relational 30–31; urban and industrial 34
site-led research 29, 119; redesign of 29; teaching strategies of 119
Siwy, K. *86*
Skype 39
Smith, A. 69
social memory 67–70
sound recordings 19
space(s) 44n5; conception of 43; conceptualisation of 30; creative/worship 95; interior and exterior 62; material 54; physical and digital 31; private and public 66; production 34; translocal relations of 31; urban 30; urban micro-utopian 63; visible and invisible systems of 35; volumetric 65
spatial design 3, 10, 27
Spivak, G. 108
Spuybroek, L. 65
Steel, C. 33
stereotomy 58
Stone, S. 2
stop-motion animation 13, 32
"Storefront for Art and Architecture, Concept and Experience" *22*
The Storm of Creativity (Leski) 2
Strayer, A. *70*
studio 20; pedagogy 4; remote 53; space of 12; structure of 11; workshop 11

Style in the Technical and Tectonic Arts: or Practical Aesthetics (Semper) 58
sugar wonderland *36*
sustainable architectural design 107
sustainable design 6, 22, 102, 103, 106, 107
Switzerland 82, *83*

Tadao Ando's Meditation Space 84
Taylor, B. 68
teaching: design studio 2; scholarship of 4; sustainable design 6
tea plantations, architectures of *37*
tectonics 58, 60, 61, 65
territorial boundary 56–60
The Museum of Art 93, 112
Therme Vals 82, *83*
Thomas Jefferson University 84, *86*, *92*, *94*
three-dimensional software 88
time-based representation 11, 19–20
topography 3, 55, 60, 120
tranquility pods 5, 84, 88, 89, 91, 93
translocal relations, spaces of 31
Tuck, E. 111

Uncommon Ground (Leatherbarrow) 3
"University Metro Station, Site Section" *23*
urban generation 103–105
urban planning 29, 31, 32, 38, 40
urban studies 30

Vaal, C. *66*
visual culture 6, 38, 40, 51

WalkingStick, K. 111
Wang, J. *18*
Western painting 107
Western visual culture 107
West/non-West art 107–110
Williams, B. *70*
Wilson, M. 5

Yao, D. *70*

Zhang, J. *103*, 104
Zoom 39, 41, 113
Zumthor, P. 82

For Product Safety Concerns and Information please contact our EU representative GPSR@taylorandfrancis.com
Taylor & Francis Verlag GmbH, Kaufingerstraße 24, 80331 München, Germany

www.ingramcontent.com/pod-product-compliance
Lightning Source LLC
Chambersburg PA
CBHW051752230426
43670CB00012B/2252